UP FRONT

UP FRONT

MY AUTOBIOGRAPHY

KERRY DIXON

WITH HARRY HARRIS

WITH FOREWORDS BY FRANK LAMPARD, PAT NEVIN AND HARRY REDKNAPP

JOHN BLAKE

Published by John Blake Publishing Limited,
3 Bramber Court, 2 Bramber Road,
London W14 9PB, England

www.johnblakebooks.com

www.facebook.com/johnblakebooks
twitter.com/jblakebooks

First published in hardback in 2016

ISBN: 978-1-78606-111-9

British Library Cataloguing-in-Publication Data:
A catalogue record for this book is available from the British Library.

Design by www.envydesign.co.uk

Printed in Great Britain by CPI Group (UK) Ltd

1 3 5 7 9 10 8 6 4 2

Papers used by John Blake Publishing are natural, recyclable products made from wood grown in sustainable forests. The manufacturing processes conform to the environmental regulations of the country of origin.

CONTENTS

ACKNOWLEDGEMENTS

Special thanks to Mum, Dad and sister Jane, also to Michele for putting up with me for thirty years, my children Gemma, Kelly and Joe, and to all relatives and friends who have helped me throughout my life and football career. Thanks, Joe, for picking me up from prison with Kim, that was a wonderful feeling!

I'd also like to thank Ron Fullbrook, Brendan McNally, Maurice Evans, John Neal, Bobby Campbell and, yes, Ken Bates, even though I left the Bridge just a handful of goals short of Bobby Tambling's all-time scoring record!

More recently, though, I have been looking for another chance after all 'the good, the bad and the football' that has coloured my life in so many shades. To that end I want to show my appreciation to Chelsea chairman Bruce Buck and benefactor Roman Abramovich for their support and understanding, Professional Footballers Association's Bobby

Barnes, who visited me in prison, David Pleat, my manager at Luton, who sent a supportive letter with Perry Groves, Steve Surridge of Eclipse Sports Promotions Ltd, who helped get me some work with personal appearances at lunches and dinners and for always being a great bloke; former World Cup team-mate Alvin Martin, who gave me some almighty stick at my first public appearance. (I missed that sort of banter, so thanks Alvin!) All showed me massive support at a time I needed it the most.

True friends: Les Harriott, Mick Justin, Denis Diggin, and Eddie Woods. It's been a long journey from school. Also Dave Blanchett, Nigel Domenique, Gary O'Reilly and Neil Barnett. Thanks for still being with me.

Finally, I cannot leave out the Harris family: journalists Harry and Linda Harris for helping me to write my life story, and their daughter Poppy for the picture taken at Pazzia in Sunningdale (venue for a number of writing sessions). Plus everyone at Blake Publishing Ltd – John Blake, editor Toby Buchan and finance director Joanna Kennedy. Also Jane Moore and Caroline for your support as always. The Tanner family from Chatham in Kent, brilliant all of you. Mick from Gillingham for helping us both while in prison. Cas Knight for great support. Julie Carr, for massive help while in prison.

Dave Folb of Lashings. Thank you for everything in the last few years. Mark Wyeth and James, my legal team – we can't win them all, thanks for everything.

And a special thank you to Kim who is in this with me and, without who, I undoubtedly would have struggled. The support, and love, has been great, and hopefully it can be paid back time and time again over the future years.

Christian Seunig from Austria, Bobby Barnes of the PFA and Mickey Bennett.

To all the people who wrote letters and sent them while I was in prison.

Ralph Varle, thanks for all the help over the years. Mick Colquhoun (my cousin), who has been great before, during, and after my time in jail.

To Andy Clark of Oakray. Thank you for giving me work when I so needed it.

To Lenny and John of Oakray, for helping me settle in there.

All CFC supporters for still believing.

FOREWORD
BY FRANK LAMPARD

Believe me, scoring nearly two hundred goals for one club is hard. It takes huge talent, commitment, dedication, the will to play through pain, the belief to keep going when everything turns against you.

And I guess that's what this book is about. The belief to keep going when everything seems to turn against you. I think this is a lesson in life for us all, and not just in football.

I got to know Kerry well when I started closing in on his 193 goals total at Chelsea. He was always generous in his attitude to me, encouraging, appreciative of how I played. My father would tell me many times that Kerry had approached him during games and spoke so positively about me, no matter how I was performing. I always appreciated that support. He was just a real football fella and became more than a Chelsea colleague to me, also a good friend.

But I can understand how the buzz of that goalscoring life

can be missed when it's gone. We can sometimes take things for granted on the pitch but life is much more than that. Now some things have gone wrong in his life, and there's been some heavy cost for him and for other people as a result.

The Kerry I know would want to put that right. He'd want to get back to that life where he can have a laugh and love his football. For all the drinking and gambling and everything else, that's his bottom line: have a laugh, love football. Nothing complicated. I can really relate to that.

It's like his game used to be. Nothing complicated. Get the ball in the area, he'd put it in the net. Pass it early, goal! Cross it, climb and head, goal!

There's a lot of Chelsea people like me who have been blessed to meet Kerry when he's been in the football environment in which he thrives. I hope his life can focus back on that. I believe writing this book can help, and I have huge respect for him in talking so candidly about his life.

And I look forward to the next chapter.

FOREWORD

BY PAT NEVIN

My earliest memories of Kerry came when he joined Chelsea, just a few short days after me. We were already at pre-season training in Aberystwyth when he strolled in, probably not carrying quite the level of confidence he affected. It was the dawn of a new era at the club, though we didn't know that at the time. Nigel Spackman, Joe McLaughlin and Eddie Niedzwiecki were other new boys and we were all out to impress in our own ways.

He might not have sparkled on the long-distance runs along the beach but everywhere else he quickly showed his class. I realised in that first week that he was deadly in the air at the back post, I never forgot that and it led to quite a few goals. Then his passion for scoring shone through, while his knack of being in the right place at the right time, the power of his shot and his timing enabled him to score all sorts of goals from all angles.

His pace was as impressive as any of those other gifts. Oddly he didn't look that fast and it often came as a shock to defenders when he opened up and blazed away from them. No one at our club could get near him in any sprints from twenty to a hundred yards. In short, he was pretty close to the perfect centre-forward.

He was also tall, blond, good-looking and soon to be an England striker. In fact, with all that going for him you would think he would be easy to hate! The thing is, though, that you couldn't dislike the Golden Boy because there didn't seem to be a bad bone in his body.

As everyone now knows there were problems underneath with addiction, which he will talk about here. He kept it well hidden in those early years; many of the players liked a flutter and he seemed no different, but we all know that for some it becomes a bigger problem because it is an illness.

There was one occasion that Kerry might have forgotten. He asked me for a loan of £200, which was a lot of money for me then but I knew it took a lot for him to ask me. I said I would go to the bank and get it for him after training. I did just that and came back knowing there was no guarantee I would see it again soon, if ever. I went to hand it over and he said 'No, just keep it Pat,' and walked away. That must have taken a huge amount of self-control, if he really needed it. I admired his fighting spirit then and there. I know it has been a fight ever since, one that will never stop but can be won only on a day-to-day basis.

Kerry still managed to have a phenomenal career; the goals flowed and he became unquestionably a Chelsea legend. Whatever you do in life, if you can say that you are a Chelsea legend then that it is something of which to be eternally proud.

FOREWORD
BY HARRY REDKNAPP

Kerry Dixon was a great goal-scorer, a really good centre-forward, a player I thoroughly enjoyed watching in his prime. But he played in an era when a club's history meant something to the players: it was special.

These days, with the huge influx of players from overseas, the clubs' traditions don't count for so much. They make their own history.

The turnover of players is so high at clubs that it doesn't matter, and half of them don't know what happened five years ago, let alone the real history, the importance of clubs' traditions; let's face it a lot of the foreign players wouldn't even be interested in that history. If you talked about Arsenal's Double-winning team of 1971, or Kerry Dixon at Chelsea, they wouldn't have a clue. They come in, they play, and they move on in a few years.

But Kerry is Chelsea through and through. He loved the club, and for that reason the fans loved him – and still do. They remember their own, and he was one of their own. Now he has fallen on hard times he needs our help, the help of people inside the game, and I am only too willing to give it.

Most people need help from time to time in their lives, and when that happens they find out who their friends are, more so at times like these than any other.

Kerry's life story is a great read, and I also hope that the books helps him back along the road to recover from all his troubles. He needs all the support he can get right now, and I am happy to support him.

CHAPTER ONE

INTRODUCTION

I think of myself as a caring, nice bloke.

I've done my share of charity work, as most footballers do, for they want to put something back and I wanted to do the same. I love my mum and dad, and respect them, too; I love my kids and all those closest to me, my sister, my family, and I want them all to be proud of me.

There have been times when they were proud of me, when I was at the peak of my playing career, scoring goals for fun for Chelsea and putting on that England shirt, playing with and against some of the world's greatest players and going to the World Cup finals. My passion, even obsession, has been scoring goals and I just wish my obsessive nature had not spread to gambling.

It's impossible to describe the elation that scoring brings. I felt that adrenalin rush whether I was scoring in the streets, the local park, the school team or in the Aztec stadium in

Mexico. I've been elated by the most simple tap-in as much as the most spectacular strikes. That's why I didn't give the game up until the game gave me up. That was the force that drove me on to continue playing until I was forty-four.

As you will discover as I unburden myself of the mishaps that have blighted my life, there have been times when those closest to me have not been proud of me, and for good reason. I want to make them proud of me again and that is one of the compelling reasons for writing this autobiography. I want to turn my life around, and use this book to draw a line under my past.

I want people to remember me as Kerry Dixon the footballer, so this book features my exploits on the field – scoring goals for club and country, playing the glorious game and how it inspired me but also telling what went on behind the scenes. Some things, I imagine, might surprise and even shock you. I want to say what it was like being a so-called superstar in the 1980s and 1990s at Stamford Bridge and other clubs I played for.

I was on a legal high, scoring goals – that was what I lived for. I didn't live for taking drugs, gambling, suffering business failures or for going to prison. But I also want to get the dark side of my life off my chest and draw a line under it. Yes, I want to remember the football, but I also hope that the rest can be laid to rest for good.

I want people to know that, in reality, I haven't changed. I'm the same person in many ways, but having suffered some painful, harsh lessons, I have learned to walk away whatever the provocation. More importantly, I have learned not put myself in a position where I am vulnerable.

INTRODUCTION

I wrote my first autobiography in my mid-twenties, when I had lived only a fraction of a life; just one side, as it turned out, of what was to happen to me. I was only a third of the way through my playing career and I was just about to go off to the World Cup in Mexico to play in the company of such iconic England superstars as Gary Lineker, John Barnes, Chris Waddle, Bryan Robson, Peter Beardsley and Peter Shilton. I was at the top of my profession at Chelsea, the club's leading scorer, the proverbial world at my feet, earning a small fortune, comparatively, for the times, with the prospect of earning even more. Little did I know then that the top rewards for the best players in English football were a pittance compared to what they earn now, although that is not, and never will be an issue with me.

After Chelsea were promoted to the First Division at the end of the 1984 season I moved into a house of my own for a short time (one of three homes I would lose because of gambling, businesses gone bad and two bankruptcies). I was forever getting kids knocking at the front door asking for my autograph. I remember one day they asked if I would sponsor them for the number of goals they would score in a Cup Final to be played on Luton Town's ground. When they called again to collect the money – after a 1–1 draw – they asked if I would consider coaching their team, the Bramingham Spitfires, the following season. Impressed by their politeness, I agreed, not knowing for a moment what it would entail.

I had forgotten all about it when some time later, there came another knock on my door. It was the kids' manager, Doug Roe, who said their season began on the following Sunday – a most inconvenient time as Chelsea's season was already under way. Still, I went to watch them play in their first friendly and was pleasantly surprised when they won 3–0. I arranged a couple of training sessions with them.

Working with those lads provided me with so much pleasure, and later in life I tried my luck in coaching and management with incredible consequences, which I will detail later in this book. Doug's wife Jan was then club secretary and they were such nice people it was a pleasure to be involved with the boys and the team. I told my Bramingham boys to be totally single-minded about goal-scoring, never to be afraid to miss and, when they got one goal, always to look for another and another.

Thinking back to that time of youthful optimism it is incredible to find a page from that first autobiography of 1986:

> The money I have earned from football has enabled me to buy a lovely house of my own; that is my security and hopefully I will have enough money to pay the mortgage off by the time I have finished playing football.

As it turned out I lost that home and two others as life progressed – having to sell up or finding myself unable to afford the rent. In the end I lost everything, up to and including my liberty, and would eventually come out of prison as I went into it: penniless.

Gambling was a big part of my downfall. They say gambling is a mug's game and I am one of the biggest mugs going. It is true that gambling is something of a disease in the football profession, but I went much further. Some of my experiences proved to be downright harrowing, surreal, even life-threatening like a scene from a film Vinnie Jones might star in.

It's been good to be honest about it all. I feel as though I have unburdened myself and for a very good reason; to prove that I have a future as well as a past. I want to exorcise the past by coming clean and telling the truth about my life up until now.

And do two important things. One is to say sorry for what I have done, for what I shouldn't have done and for what I regret I have done.

The second thing is even harder: to work relentlessly to become a better person and to learn from my mistakes. That's not to say I agree that I should be provoked, abused and insulted just because I am a 'face' who happens to be in a public place, but I am learning to walk away from provocation.

As I have said, I intend this book to mark the point at which I turn my life around and once again make my parents and my loved ones proud of me. I can do that by helping myself, and I am lucky enough to know that there are those who want to help me. I plan not to let them down.

CHAPTER ONE

LIKE FATHER, LIKE SON

I was born in Luton, in Bedfordshire, on 24 July 1961, into a Victorian house in Oak Road, just a free kick away from Kenilworth Road, the ground of Luton Town FC, our local football club. My dad, Mick Dixon, was a professional footballer at the club at that time, but I don't think he got more than one game as a centre-forward before he moved on. Dad moved clubs a lot, playing for Coventry City as well as various non-league teams, so that meant a lot of moving around for the family in my first few years. We eventually ended up back in Luton at a house in Bodmin Road when I was almost three years old, and stayed at that house until I was eighteen.

I'm often asked about my unusual name. It was Mum's idea, and she stuck to it despite some formidable opposition from Dad. I didn't like it too much either when I got a bit older, and once told the family I intended to change it to Michael when I got could. Thank goodness I didn't, for the name, although more common nowadays, is distinctive, and over the years has proved to be a great asset, not least in grabbing the headlines. I can't recall another footballer with the same name. Mum tells me the name came from an Australian athlete she saw running in a steeplechase race. He fell at one of the hurdles and maybe she felt sorry for him, for the name Kerry O'Brien stuck in her mind. Later, she was returning by train from London with my dad and there was a lad in the compartment whose name was Kerry. It was then she said that if the baby she was carrying was a boy she intended to call him Kerry.

In time I grew comfortable with the name, and actually rather like it. If the letters from fans at the height of my career with Chelsea and England were anything to go by then the name become more popular. Many wrote to me saying they intended to call their kids Kerry.

Football was in my DNA, and the earliest memory I have is of kicking a ball about in the garden with my dad. His footballing skills were passed down to me, of that I am sure. He would throw the ball to me and I would kick it as hard as I could, left foot and right foot, loving every minute of it. It is clear to me now that my dad was trying to get me to use both feet, knowing how being two-footed would be a great advantage . But it was predominantly the right foot I would hit the ball with, feeling far more comfortable. As the years went by the left foot became my 'swinger'. Dad kept on encouraging me to use my left foot if need be, even though he could see it was never going to be as comfortable for me, nor would I be as accurate, using my right foot.

Being a player himself, his advice if the ball fell on my left side, was to take a chance and strike it, ensuring it was on target as I might not get a chance if I were to use up precious seconds switching feet.

That I was football-mad from an early age absolutely delighted him. Other kids were into model aeroplanes, tool kits and toy cars but I was never interested in that kind of stuff; I was just happy with a ball. Running was my other strength and Dad encouraged me all the way but my greatest passion by far was football, and especially the thrill of scoring goals.

Both my parents have always been totally supportive. My mum, Anne, was the backbone of the home for me and my sister Jane, she and Dad were right behind me when it came to sport. He used to come and watch me play in as many school matches as he could. I remember him standing on the touchline in his overcoat in the pouring rain, cheering me on. He would take time off work to come and support me, and has always been there throughout my life. I have so much respect for my parents who, even now, will still tick me off when I've done something wrong. Unfortunately, there has been a lot of ticking off along the way.

I am lucky though, in that I have always enjoyed a close-knit relationship with my family. Jane, my sister, would go on to provide assistance during my football career and well beyond it. Something of a tomboy in her younger days, she was always willing to play the goalkeeper if I wanted to practise my shooting.

Later on, when I was working in an engineering factory, Dad would get me out of bed at 6.00 a.m. to report for football practice in a field at the back of the house. That may sound a touch uncivilised, but those are memories that I will treasure. Indeed, without the assistance of my family the chances are I would not have become a successful footballer. They also prevented me from playing the big star at the height of my career, for the fact that I spent a great deal of time at home with my parents meant that my feet were always firmly on the ground. Mum would give me a clip around the ear if I ever got above myself. I went on to take some wrong turns in life, but I would have been far worse off without the total commitment and support of my family.

In turn, I went to watch Dad play, mostly non-league football at clubs such as Bedford, Biggleswade and Bletchley. Invariably I spent my time finding a bit of space behind the goal and kicking the ball around, imagining that I was actually playing out there with my dad.

As I got bigger my Dad kept up his habit of kicking the ball around with me in the garden, making up a goal with jumpers, and then I progressed to playing in the streets. You don't see much of that these days and many commentators have made the point that kids are no longer practising and honing their skills by endless hours playing in the streets as we would do in our era. They have so much more these days to occupy their minds, such as the computer games smartphones and social media that keep them indoors and so much less active when they could be playing football with their mates. Of course, the roads are far busier than they were in my day, and I also benefited from living in a cul-de-sac. And I guess it would be unfair to say kids don't want to kick a ball around with their mates at all. These days I see plenty of them in the local parks, but more often than not they are playing organised games and the kids are in their kit rather than enjoying the impromptu kickabouts we used to have in our jeans and trainers.

In my road there were ten or twelve kids who would congregate to kick the ball around and there were plenty of girls in that group who wanted to play football with us. One of my mates, Les Harriott, with whom I often spent time kicking the ball around in the streets and the park, remains one of my closest friends to this day.We'd put jumpers down for goalposts or someone's double drive would do for one of the goals. The pitch would usually be at a light angle, but we didn't care. I was quite popular as invariably it was my ball we used.

We all lived for football in our street; we couldn't get enough of it. But sometimes we got too much of it as far as some of our neighbours were concerned. The ball would hit a door, or end up in someone's back garden. One woman grew especially sick of us, and would complain whenever the ball was kicked into her hedge or, worse still, ended up in her back garden. She got so fed up that she would keep the ball and once she threatened to burst it if it ever came into her garden again. She was a bit of a battle-axe or so it seemed to us kids. Now I would say she had every right to be fed up with us, considering how often the ball ended up in her garden and, of course, it was usually I who had to go to retrieve it.

One day my mum had to go to fetch my precious ball back, after the neighbour kicked up a particularly big fuss and refused to return it. It seemed that Mum was on my side when that happened, but far from it. I might have got the ball back but I also got a right bollocking afterwards and from then onwards our group had to go a little further to the local park for our kickabouts. But, although we never had a lot of money when I was growing up, there was always enough to buy me a new football when I needed it.

CHAPTER TWO

RUTHLESS AND COMPETITIVE – FAILED AT LUTON AND SPURS

As a kid I was slight, rather than the muscular centre-forward I would become in my prime. My mum reckoned that between the ages of eleven and fourteen I didn't grow at all. But I was a determined little so-and-so who just couldn't stand the thought of being beaten at anything. From that point, throughout my football career, I had that same obsessive streak, a ruthless, competitive edge that took me to the top in football, but also to the bottom in my life.

It did seem from an early age that I had an aptitude for sport – most sports, really, but I excelled at rugby and especially football. I would say I was actually quite a good rugby player and though not overly quick at an early age I got faster as I got older and stronger.

I represented Beechwood junior school at all sports at one time or another and went on to represent the county,

Bedfordshire, at rugby and football. I was in the school teams for the year above my age when I discovered that knack of scoring goals. In those early days, Les Harriot played in the same school team as I did. The captain, a boy named Wayne Turner, went on to play for Coventry and become assistant manager at Luton under David Pleat.

The previous leading scorer at my school managed thirteen goals in just over twenty games and I wanted to break that record. I did so within a month, and scored sixty-six goals as a ten-year-old. I also played for Sunday team Dunstable Claymores, Luton Boys' Club and Lewsey Centre.

As I progressed, doing well for whichever team I played in, Dad kept a low profile, out of the way of team managers. I appreciated that approach. It was embarrassing to see how some dads pushed their boys – often beyond the point of reasonable behaviour.

I certainly had my heroes and role models when I was growing up, as many, if not all the kids had in those days. Football was the number one preoccupation of a kid's thoughts. No PlayStations, Xboxes or social media non-stop on their smartphones in those days. I watched Luton Town as a kid during the days when they were in the Fourth Division.

I can remember watching Malcolm Macdonald play for Luton when I was just a kid, standing on the terraces and being amazed by his electrifying pace, lethal shots and considerable heading ability. The supporters loved him. I loved him. He excited them and he excited me. He once scored all five goals for England against Cyprus, but still his critics insisted he couldn't play. Even so, it is not without significance that goal-scorers are the most highly-prized commodity in the game.

While 'Super Mac' was a favourite player, it was predominantly the Luton team as a whole that inspired me rather than any one individual. The team had so many good players at that time. I would go along to the Kenilworth Road stadium with my mates and stand on the terraces at the Oak Road end.

I cannot recall how much it cost to get in – maybe the equivalent of 5p today. Mum and Dad always found the money for me to go to watch football, and they'd scrape together the coins I needed for the double-decker bus ride there and back, too. I loved to watch the likes of Ron and Paul Futcher, Alan West, Jimmy Ryan, John Aston and Barry Butlin and Vic Halom, a centre-forward who also played for Sunderland.

I was just as happy watching football on *Match of the Day*, presented in those days by Jimmy Hill. Watching... playing– football was my life. But while I loved to go and watch the games, I preferred to play. Somehow I always scored a lot of goals. I just seemed to have the knack for scoring rather than playing in any other position. That didn't happen only by being inspired by strikers. I just loved scoring goals as it sort of came naturally to me. I worked hard over the years and did so even when I made it to the top, to improve my touch and technique, but although I think it is very important to work hard at overcoming your shortcomings, it is even more vital to work at what you are good at.

Ian Rush was the finest exponent of the art of goal-scoring in my formative years. He also had the ability to hold up the ball and bring colleagues into play; the complete frontman. Yet he too had his critics early on, determined to find fault, search out his weaknesses and focus on them rather than applaud him for what he was a master at doing. 'Ah, he cannot head the ball!' – that was one of the negatives thrown in his direction. Yet I've seen Rushy score some superb goals with his head.

As I grew older, the next stop for me was Challney secondary school. I also joined Luton Boys' Club – that was where I met Les Harriott and two other valued mates, Mick Justin and Eddie Woods. Les and I were selected for Luton Town's schoolboy team. There were better players than me I in that team and the scouts from the big clubs were watching closely.

There were some decent footballers at Luton, some of whom made it to the top. It was fun and I loved it, but I did gain a reputation for being a bit of a moaner on the field and giving my teammates some stick at times. This was a reflection of my ruthless, competitive streak. I was also a bit of a rebel when I thought I could get away it. I once missed just one training session to have a night out at a disco with my mates and I got on the wrong side of Dave Morton, coach of the schoolboy team. He kicked me out. I failed to take on board that I was in the wrong, but then again that was my attitude as a teen. I was stubborn and determined. If I didn't think something was right I wasn't shy in coming forward and saying so. If that's rebelliousness, then that is what I was, rebellious.

In Sunday football, I moved on from Luton Boys to Lewsey Centre in the Chiltern League, where Ron Fullbrook was in charge. I also represented the county of Bedfordshire, scoring a record one hundred and sixty-seven goals that season, mainly because I was playing so many games. In a way I'd got my revenge on Mr Morton for kicking me out of the Luton schoolboy team.

Ron Fullbrook, a good guy and a great character, taught me an awful lot about life. I'm not sure he knew a lot about football but that wasn't his forte; he worked tirelessly helping under-privileged kids in the Lewsey community centre. He gave many who really needed it sound advice, including me. He taught me that you need to keep your spirits high even when things are not going your way, and that you have to remember there are many, many people far worse off than you. If you think you've got a problem, see what some people have to go through, and yet they just get on with it. He taught me how to get on with my life when the knocks came my way, and there were plenty of knocks in my early days when I was trying to get on to the football ladder.

I once scored thirteen goals in a 16–1 win. It was my Sunday team – I played both Saturdays and Sundays as football was all-consuming. Sam Berry, a good friend of mine at the time, was playing in the other team, and it would be fair to say they didn't play at all well rather than that we were that brilliant. I was always single-minded when it came to goal-scoring. At times it would work against me for some accused me of being greedy; however, it was a bit much when I scored those thirteen goals when they forced me to play in goal to keep me out of the way! The goalkeeper had to go off and I think the manager was being tongue-in-cheek when he stuck me in goal. He probably felt it would even things up between the two team as we were so far ahead it was making a nonsense of the game as a competitive match. But I hated being in goal, standing around, particularly as were so much on top, and I don't think I touched the ball. I'm not saying I did a huge amount of running around when I played up front, but just standing between the sticks wasn't for me, and I was never to play in goal again.

My dad took the games almost as seriously as I did –, perhaps even more so. If I'd played well and popped in a couple of goals, all was peace and harmony in the Dixon household, but when he thought I could have done better he grounded me. My sister Jane would sometimes waylay me before I could get into the house. 'Did you score? Did you play well?' If the answer was a 'No,' Jane's face would give away how she guessed the rest of the day might go. 'Oh, God' she'd say, 'I don't want to go inside the house.'

Dad did mellow eventually, but we still had our arguments over my performances. But he's always been my greatest supporter as well as my strongest critic. The trouble was, he was rarely wrong. It's often thought that the more your parents try to tell you things, the more you rebel against them. And while I did have a rebellious streak, I tended to listen to the advice from my parents, particularly from Dad because of his background.

Yet even as I was being ticked off about my playing, I tended to act the rebel, and say to myself that I didn't give a toss what anyone said, because I was young enough to think I knew best. Of course, I didn't. Because Dad was right far more often than not, it was easier just to listen and accept his advice and criticism when it was justified.

From the age of eleven, I trained with Luton Town FC when David Pleat, who went on to manage Spurs, was the manager and Danny Bergara coached the kids. My ambition was to play for my home-town club, and some years later I got into their youth team and at that time thought I was on the way to making it. Once I went on a as sub, but after five minutes Pleat and Bergara took me off – shame, anger, bewilderment: you can imagine how I felt.

I went over to my dad, who was watching by the touchline, in tears, confused. He was also surprised at the way a fifteen-year-old schoolboy had been treated. We stood watching the rest of the game and then he advised me to go back to the dressing room with the rest of the team, even though I felt sick inside. I didn't speak in the dressing room and nobody spoke to me either.

The following week I was not one of the subs – I was in the team itself. So fathom that one out – I can't. I don't even recall how the game turned out. I had really lost interest by then. I had been training with Luton after school in the evenings and before the spring half-term David Pleat had told us that during the school holidays we were welcome to report to Kenilworth Road. Kenilworth Road meant something special to me as the home ground of my home-town team. It still means a lot to me as I live in the area and I have fond memories of the place. It was pretty antiquated at the time when I trained there and it hasn't changed that much over the years, despite a few improvements – nothing special. At least it's still standing. The town should have a new stadium – the supporters deserve it and the club needs it.

I went to the ground on the Tuesday and Wednesday but didn't bother on the Thursday and, after watching the first team on the Saturday with my mates, I was waiting for a bus with Les when Pleat came walking by and asked why I hadn't turned up on the Thursday. I blustered an excuse that I had had to go out with my mum, and Pleat muttered that I might discover I would have plenty more time to go out with my mum if I didn't watch out.

Six weeks later the club issued registration forms for the players they had chosen to keep as apprentices. We were a good youth team that year and all – a record sixteen – got signed on. All except two. Yes, you've guessed it: I was one of them. I was devastated. I tried to pretend I was a big shot and didn't care but the feeling of nausea wouldn't go away. Mum was supportive but Dad, who wasn't one for platitudes, told me that perhaps I wasn't good enough. I was starting to learn some harsh life lessons early on.

The other reject was a lad called John Mawhinney. Our rejection was sickening for both of us, and there and then I made up my mind to become a toolmaker and play non-league football. Yet I still ended that season as top scorer for the youth team, even though I didn't play in all the games. But the incident when I was taken off after five minutes, alongside my rejection, left scars that never healed. Of course, it was a kick in the teeth at the time but you learn from life experiences like that, as my dad said, and in the end the setback didn't stop me.

I received a letter from Luton informing me that they believed it was the correct decision not to offer me an apprenticeship but they were willing to sign me as an amateur so they could play me in their teams on a Saturday as part of the 'satellite squad'. They invited me to Kenilworth Road for a chat, but I didn't see the point. It was such a comedown and I wasn't going to be second-best, training on the off-chance something might turn up.

I bumped into Danny Bergara and he told me not to feel too

downhearted and to take inspiration from Luton player Ricky Hill. Ricky was someone I rated very highly, who eventually went on to play for England after having been denied apprentice forms. He made the grade coming through as an amateur. Danny tried to persuade me to sign amateur forms, and prove everyone wrong about me. If I took this course of action I might improve my game with the experience. I declined. Maybe it was my pride getting in the way, but sometimes you have to make those sorts of decisions in life, and that was mine. You either stand or fall by the decision, but at least I had the support of my mum and dad.

Brendan McNally, who had played for Luton as a full-back in the 1959 FA Cup Final against Nottingham Forest, was manager of Chesham United in the Isthmian League, and at the age of sixteen I went along to train with them. Despite my confidence having been dealt a sever blow at Luton, he picked me as sub for the first team on several occasions and I finally got my chance when Chesham were 4–1 down at Hornchurch and the manager took off centre-forward Jim McCarthy with twenty-five minutes to go.

Jim stormed toward the touchline, flinging his shirt on the ground. Gordon Taylor, the assistant manager, was playing in midfield and told me not to worry but to play my normal game. Gordon scored and I popped one in to make it 4–3 and I can still recall the sheer excitement at hitting the equaliser. Just before the end we also got a winner. I became a regular and the goals flowed, while poor Jim lost his No. 9 place to me. There was little or no place for sympathy, however. It was a hard road to get to where you wanted to be in this game. Jim was an experienced pro and he knew the score. He would not have expected an arm around his shoulder from me, and it might not even have felt genuine had he got it. I was a teenager trying to make his way in the game and that was how it was, and it probably hasn't changed much since. Jim opted to switch to centre-half and I later played in the same team with him at Dunstable, and he is perfectly fine about how it all turned out.

I left school at fifteen with four O-levels. My dad advised me to get a job and I took an apprenticeship with local firm, Cardale Engineering, as a toolmaker. As part of the apprenticeship, I attended Dunstable College to study for a Higher National Diploma (HND) in Engineering. College and now work and football – it was hectic but enjoyable.

Maurice Walby was a workmate of my mum's and a scout for Tottenham who said he could arrange for me to have a trial. I jumped at the chance. Spurs were a massive club at the time – and still are, of course. Ron Henry was then coaching the kids and he had been part of their famous Double-winning side of 1961. Peter Shreeves, who went on to become manager, was in charge of the reserves and helped Ron with the youth teams. Bill Nicholson was still in the background with Keith Burkinshaw as manager, and they had plenty of big stars.

I was shocked when I was told I had been recommended by Maurice. I thought my opportunity with the game had gone – to be given a second chance and at such a major club took my breath away. I was determined to give it all that I could. John Mawhinney, the other kid rejected with me at Luton, was also given a trial. Spurs seemed impressed with us both and it wasn't long before I was scoring for Spurs' youth team in a 3–1 win.

Spurs' youth team were involved in a cup final over two legs against Oxford United. John and I didn't play in the first game, which Spurs lost 4–1 and we had little chance of playing in the second one. But we were picked for the second leg to play alongside the likes of Mark Falco, Gary O'Reilly, Giorgio Mazzon and Garry Brooke, with John playing up front alongside Falco and me. I scored twice in a 4–0 win. I was very pleased with myself. Offered apprentice forms, I went and had a serious chat with Dad. He was concerned I would have one year in which to impress Spurs and that this would pose a huge risk. I would have to give up my job and leave college with nothing left to fall back on if it all went pear-shaped at Spurs. It was always at the back of my mind that I would be rejected again. You could hardly blame me after what happened at Luton. The deal-breaker was that Spurs were not offering me a full-time contract.

Dad and I both came to the conclusion that it would be wise to reject the offer. Peter Shreeves was marvellous. He said he understood our decision and applauded me for being so sensible. He was prepared to make me a part-time professional so I could still play for Spurs and complete my apprenticeship at the toolmakers. Mick Burrows – my boss there– was accommodating, as it meant I had to leave work a couple of hours early when I had to get to Spurs. It was agreed that I could work late other nights, which I did, although it proved to be a tough, exhausting existence.

Dad would pick me up in his car from work to rush me off to the railway station. I would travel to London and catch a tube to Seven Sisters before walking to White Hart Lane just in time for training at 7.00 p.m. Ron Henry was in charge of the training but Peter Shreeves was always in attendance. Sometimes we'd catch a glimpse of manager Keith Burkinshaw and his assistant Pat Welton, as well as the great Bill Nicholson, who was scouting for new players after his magnificent career as manager at Spurs. Ron Henry was a super fellow. He used to give me a lift back home to Luton after training, and told great stories of his exploits with the illustrious team of 1961.

I loved it at Spurs. The dressing-room banter was lively and there were some great lads. We won the South-East Counties League and I scored more than thirty goals in the season, although my mate John was released halfway through the season. It was his second knock-back after Luton. The two of us had enjoyed our time together, travelling around in luxury coaches and mixing with great players. But we never discussed his departure. We left each other to sort out our lives ourselves. In reality, there was nothing to say, nothing we could do for each other; it was how it was. In those days, everyone accepted their fate and never moaned about it. You got used to it, particularly if you suffered rejection more than once.

John went on to become an architect, and I was determined to finish my apprenticeship as a toolmaker. I needed to learn that trade as a career playing football was proving to be so precarious. Even so, the time seemed to fly by. In a way it would have been harder if Spurs had offered me a full-time contract but as it was I was already, aged eighteen, in the third year of a four-year apprenticeship.

It was nerve-racking and tense when the time came for Spurs to decide who was going to stay on. Fellow youth-team player

Jez Reardon hadn't even waited to be told and had already cleared off to the States. (In 1986 I would have a pleasant surprise while out in LA with the England squad, the year before the World Cup in Mexico, when somebody came up to me and said that Jez had asked to be remembered to me.) For my part, I also feared the worst for my own future at Spurs. I was doing reasonably well, having scored thirty-two goals and finished as top scorer. It was certainly enough to earn me a full-time place. I knew I would have to give an offer very serious consideration. Chris Hughton was a year or so ahead of me, playing regularly in the reserves and beginning to break into the first team, but he too was concluding his studies and had a tough decision to make even though he had made the first team.

One night after training Peter Shreeves asked me to stay back so he could have a private word with me. He said he had bad news. He didn't say any more at first, but I'll never forget the way he handled a very delicate situation, a traumatic moment in the life of an ambitious young man. He explained that Tottenham were not going to take me on as a full-time professional. At Spurs the policy was for a committee to reach a decision on the future of a player and in my case it had been by Keith Burkinshaw, Pat Welton, Bill Nicholson, Ron Henry and Shreeves himself. Peter said I had presented them with a very difficult decision – one of the most difficult they had had to reach – so the vote must have been close.

He continued: 'As yet we don't know about you. We feel we are not prepared to take a chance. It was a split decision and the manager was forced to exercise a casting vote. I would like you to know that Ron Henry and I wanted to take a chance. We have seen you the most and you have scored a lot of goals, and we believe you could score those goals in the reserve team'.

I was approaching my eighteenth birthday, and my age probably counted against me. Although I made a couple of Football Combination League reserve appearances for Spurs, the competition for places was intense. It was even more intense in my position, as there was an abundance of strikers, including Peter Taylor, who went on to play for England, Gerry Armstrong, already a fixture in the Northern Ireland team and someone who went on to score one of the World Cup's greatest goals against Spain, Colin Lee, who went on to become a teammate at Chelsea, Ian Moores, a big strong No. 9 signed by the club for big money at the time, and home-grown Chris Jones who, although unlucky in front of goal, had a huge talent, also as a No. 9. Fellow youngsters such as Mark Falco became a first-teamer at the Lane and Terry Gibson, already emerging from the youth set-up, was eventually sold on for £90,000 to Coventry and moved on again to Manchester United.

I was naturally desperately disappointed to miss out but I could see the bigger picture from the club's perspective. But, equally, it was baffling that there was no longer any room for the youth team's highest scorer. And it was not much consolation later on to hear Peter Shreeves after he succeeded Keith Burkinshaw as manager. 'Had I possessed the managerial power I have now, Kerry Dixon would still be with the club and leading our First Division attack alongside Mark Falco,' he said. 'I thought he had done more than enough to merit being signed on a full-time basis by the club. But others did not share my belief in him, unfortunately. He has matured into a young man who has literally got the world at his feet. There are no targets he cannot attain. Provided he stays clear of injury I think we are going to see him scoring goals at the highest level for the next decade.'

I will never forget Peter Shreeves's kindness, understanding and consoling words for a young player whose ambitions had been shattered. I have always been able to relate to people who are honest and straightforward, and although, like many players, I've discovered there are a lot of two-faced people in football, Peter Shreeves was certainly not one of them. All of the young lads at Tottenham respected him. We regarded him as something special.

Shreeves dedicated his life to Spurs and did a magnificent job as he worked his way through the ranks, finally achieving his great ambition when he was appointed manager of the club. Sadly, he failed to live up to Tottenham's expectations, but I hope they will never forget the very special talents which got him there and the massive debt they owe him. All too often, in my opinion, a decent, talented coach is allowed to leave the club just because it is felt he has not quite come off as a manager.

It hurt to be kicked out by Spurs, hurt very much. In fact, I was inconsolable. Once again I turned to Dad for advice, and he was adamant that I should persevere with my engineering apprenticeship. I knew that he and Mum were so disappointed for me, but they hid it well. And in any case, it wasn't nearly as bad as the rejection I felt when it first hit me back at Luton, when I thought my dreams of football been dashed for good.

In reality, I absolutely hated the factory life and it was the football that had helped to sustain me; that was now being taken away. Being a toolmaker was a very poor second-best but it was the safe option, the one that any sensible person would have taken given the disappointments I had suffered. I never intended to give up on the game entirely and I would have enjoyed myself playing non-league football. Also, I was determined that I would complete my engineering apprenticeship even if Spurs had offered me terms. Then, in the very early 1980s, with unemployment rising, I was glad that I had a trade to fall back on.

I was studying for my technical education certificate in engineering, mathematics, pure mathematics and all of the sciences. My parents urged me to step up my studies and not get side tracked by football. A qualified toolmaker was the highest-paid job on the factory floor. They insisted that I would appreciate my good fortune later in life.

I was earning the princely sum of £35 a week at the factory and £30 a match from playing part-time for Tottenham (about £160 and £140, respectively, at today's values). This enabled me to believe I was doing very well for myself, especially as a teenager, although ever since my first pay packet Mum had taken £5 off me each week for what she called bed-and-board. In fact, she put every penny of into a bank account for me. I had no choice in the matter but I didn't mind one bit. The following year she withheld £10 a week from my wages and this, too, went into the bank account. Whenever we had an argument, she would tell me the money she'd taken was for herself – but she couldn't fool anyone. Her exercise provided a lesson in saving money that I wish I had continued to follow.

When it began to sink in that I would not be going back to Spurs, the suspicion that I was just not good enough to earn a full-time living as a professional footballer made me extremely depressed. Yet this turned out to be the last time in my entire life that I allowed myself such thoughts.

CHAPTER THREE

BREAKTHROUGH

Time for yet another heart-to-heart talk with my dad. His advice was to stay calm and see what developed. I received an offer from Leyton Orient to go on their summer tour as my reputation as a goal-scorer had impressed them, but I was unable to accept because I was working full-time in the factory.

Peter Sheeeves said he would do all he could to help me. Charlton Athletic, one of his former clubs, made me a reasonable offer. But I was disillusioned and who could blame me? I had not abandoned all hope of proving Luton and Tottenham wrong, but making the grade no longer seemed the be-all and end-all that it had been. I had taken too many knocks, suffered too many setbacks.

I seem to have a remarkable capacity for being able to shut things away, and quite soon found I was happy leading my ordinary life and enjoying socialising with my mates. My love of the game itself had not diminished in the slightest; the real problem was where and when I could play. Fortunately, a situation presented itself which was to make and decision of mine a formality. Brendan McNally, who had been manager of Chesham when I played there, was appointed manager of Dunstable Town. Despite finishing in the bottom half of the Southern First Division, the club had been upgraded to the Southern Premier League in the reorganisation caused by the introduction of the new Alliance League.

The big news for Dunstable was signing Stuart Atkins from Wycombe. I had played at Chesham with him and we forged a potent goal-scoring partnership as well as becoming friends. My dad, who was a regular at Dunstable for years, had to admit this was the best team he'd seen.

It wasn't long before Stuart and I were called up to represent the Southern League in Italy, which was quite an honour at the time. Better still, we captured the representative title with Stuart and I both scoring one each to win 2–0. I finished my season top scorer with fifty-two goals, Stuart second with thirty-seven. It did so much to restore my belief after what happened at Luton and Spurs.

I'd work all week in the factory, train twice a week and go out on Friday night, although I didn't drink in those days. Once, though, I got back home at 3a.m. and that didn't go down too well with my parents. I approached the house in dread and panic, and tried to sneak up the stairs but the light snapped on and Mum was standing there with a face like thunder. Mum and Dad had always been strict on discipline and the worst punishment was to be grounded for a week. She went absolutely bananas.

'Where have you been?' she demanded. Before I could reply

there was a stinging slap across my face as she proceeded to read the riot act. 'You have a game tomorrow, young man,' she raged. 'You are letting everybody down and you don't care, do you? It's high time you got a grip on your life. You are a disgrace. It's time you became a lot more responsible instead of thinking about nothing but discos and hanging around with your friends. Your dad has given up on you.'

I was dumbstruck. Mum shocked me. I was thinking I was doing okay – working, training and playing; hardly a slouch. But I couldn't forget the anger in her face and in her tone. I knew I had to concentrate on being good to get back into her good books and chat up Dad when I saw him after work.

The next afternoon we escaped with a draw and while I felt hard done by after the previous night's rant by Mum, I came to realise she was right. Without that kind of parental guidance behind me I would not have made it and, looking back, I must admit my attitude might have contributed to my early failures at Luton and Spurs. My parents shared my ambitions and my dread, as well as my successes and failures. They instilled in me the belief that life can't be lived just for the moment. My dad always gave me advice, much of it invaluable – once he smashed his kneecap in a game at Southampton and he used to remind me that injury can end a career in an instant.

There were rumours I read in the papers and heard from people supposedly in the know that Luton had second thoughts and wanted me back, but the talk was never substantiated. Torquay made an offer that Dunstable rejected. Then out of the blue I was told the club had accepted a bid from Third Division Reading. Having had so many slaps in the face I wasn't as excited as I might have been by the possibility of becoming a full-time professional, but Dad and I agreed we should meet with them out of courtesy. I still harboured a dream that I might become a footballer full-time. but my apprenticeship remained important to me too.

We met the Reading manager, Maurice Evans, at a pub just off the M1. He struck me immediately as a warm, friendly, honest man. He was also extremely persuasive and after a while I began to warm to the idea of giving it a go again. He stressed that Reading were making no guarantees of a place in the team, despite their ambitions, but he believed that with a few reserve games behind me I would be good enough to play in the Third Division.

I was about to enter the final year of my apprenticeship at the factory and I knew full well that things might not work out for me so I was determined to resist the temptation to sign for Reading full-time. I was approaching my nineteenth birthday and thought this could be a key decision in my life.

I explained my predicament to Maurice Evans, who was extremely sympathetic. Between us we agreed a two-year contract that would enable me to play as a part-time professional for the first season while I completed my apprenticeship with Cardale Engineering. As there was no evening training, Mick Burrows at Cardale agreed to me taking two mornings a week off work so long as I reported back to the factory at 2.00 p.m. on each occasion and made up for lost time by working until 6.00 p.m. every day. It was another fine gesture from him, and as a result the deal with Reading was finalised.

This was the first time in Dunstable's history that they had been able to sell a player directly to a Football League Club and the fee, £20,000, was a big sum in those days. It also repaid Brendan McNally's faith in me, for he had always told me I would make it.

I started the first twenty-five games for Reading before being dropped and I was then in and out of the side. Perhaps that did me good as I came back with a flurry of goals in the final ten games to establish myself as the top scorer at the club in the 1980–1 season.

My first goal in the Football League came against Brentford on 23 August 1980 in a 2-1 Reading win at Griffin Park with a simple tap-in, the sort of goal that only your nearest and dearest will remember. But I couldn't have been more elated if it had been the winning goal in the World Cup final and swore it would be the first of many. I wanted to repeat that feeling many times over.

Playing part time, though, was a nightmare. Lack of practice sessions with teammates affected the side's cohesion, understanding and team work. In addition, I was disillusioned at work, as football had now taken over my life completely. I'd had a bit of success, scored goals and now that was all I could think about.

A new charge-hand was appointed at Cardale and it wasn't long before I began to feel he was picking on me. Perhaps I annoyed him on purpose. Inevitably, we had a big row when he screamed as me one morning that I hadn't been working hard enough and I told him to get lost – except I said something stronger. It was a big mistake. A complaint was made to the works foreman and I was sacked on the spot with just eight weeks of my apprenticeship to go. I apologised profusely. I tried to explain that he had been niggling at me for six months, but it was all in vain.

It seemed that all the hard work to get as far as I had done at the factory counted for nothing, and that I would be for ever classed as an unskilled worker. When I told my parents I was given a real rollicking. I made a personal plea to Mick Burrows, who had been promoted to manager. Dad came along with me and we explained the situation. Mick was hardly sympathetic and gave me a severe dressing down, but fortunately he also said the foreman had acted hastily in sacking me on the spot. I was transferred from the tool room to the welding machines. This was still punishment but at least it wasn't a dismissal and the break allowed me to get my apprenticeship papers signed. I was a fully qualified toolmaker.

My devil-may-care attitude had to change as a footballer too. It was now or never for me if the game was to be my livelihood and I was determined to make a real go of it.

Dad left nothing to chance. He had been sympathetic when I suffered rejection at Luton and Spurs, but now he laid down the law in no uncertain terms. He gave me quite a speech and, in the main, I took his advice.

'This is your big chance to make a living out of the game. If you are going to do it, do it well. Your attitude must be nothing less than one hundred per cent from this moment on. It won't matter if you are not the highest-paid player in the world. What is important is that you aim to become a top First Division player. If you can't achieve that, then aim for being a top Second Division player, and so on. But just make sure you are good at whatever level you attain.

'It's a great life, go out and enjoy it. You'll have your fair share of fun but make damned sure you give it everything you've got. It beats working in a factory all of your life.

'Whatever you earn be sure to keep something back to rely on. The price of failure will be high. You'll spend the rest of your life haunted by what could have been achieved if you had been dedicated. Work at the game: want to win, want to succeed.'

He knew that my will to win, my burning desire to succeed no matter what the obstacles, had carried me a long way, but at the same time I was still only nineteen and had an awful lot to learn.

The initial stages of my first season as a full-time professional were not easy. I had expected to go from strength to strength after finishing top scorer with Reading as a part-timer and believed that concentrating on training would make me fitter, sharper and more experienced. After all, I'd completed the previous season with five goals in the final seven games. But I soon became anxious and concerned when the goals failed to flow. I was always a notoriously slow starter, tuning my timing and rhythm, but this pre-season it was harder than usual and I found myself in the reserves. Burning with ambition and commitment, I worked harder than ever to capture the attention of Maurice Evans.

Off the field I showed my naivety when I gave an interview to the *Reading Evening Post* with a young reporter named Russell Kempson. He wanted to write an article to mark my twentieth birthday. He suggested it would be nice to set a target of twenty goals for the season as I embarked on my full-time career. I said that I thought this sounded like a good idea, but I changed my mind when I saw 'I want twenty goals this year' in print.

I cringed with embarrassment, it sounded so boastful, so crass. I don't blame the reporter as it was very much my own fault, but in cold print I came over like a loudmouth, I thought, who had become too big for his boots. The incident provided me with a precious insight into how the media can manipulate people. I had been taught a lesson I would not forget in a hurry. In those days there was little or no advice given by the clubs about how to respond in interviews, although such training has become more important in today's multimedia world. It's easy to see, now, why some well-known managers refuse to let the media anywhere near their young players. But aged nineteen, I was an innocent abroad.

After that, I was much more careful what I said to journalists, although the local press weren't as tough as the hardened Fleet Street hacks I would later encounter. But even with the Reading press I had set myself up for a fall. I was constantly reminded about my boast of twenty goals for the season and soon the match reports written by the same journalist, Russell Kempton, were claiming, 'Dixon, who pledged to score twenty goals this season, doesn't look like achieving that target.' Thanks a lot, mate.

At the time, the emerging star of the Reading team was Neil Webb, a midfield player of considerable ability – you could see it even then. Indeed, the scouts were attracted to Reading to watch him. I completed the season with a flourish and ended up with fourteen goals in forty-four first team games. This was three behind Webb, the only time I had so far failed to be top goal-scorer. In my final game we beat Gillingham 2–1 and I began to feel much more comfortable with the pace, technique and skills levels required in the Football League. I played so well in the Gillingham match that their manager, Keith Peacock, tried to sign me that summer.

By the end of the season my basic wage was just £120 a week with bonuses of £40 for a win and £20 for a draw (about £465, £155 and £77 in today's money). To put that in context, I could have made more by working as a toolmaker and playing part-time non-league. Yet that was the least of my problems. My two-year contract with Reading expired in 1982 with no sign of it being extended.

I reported for pre-season with my future in limbo. It was at that point that Keith Peacock made his move, saying he had been sufficiently impressed with my performance against his team to meet me for talks about being signed for Gillingham. We met at a London hotel and I found him a very likeable sort of person, full of enthusiasm and optimism about the future of his side. He offered me £220 a week, £100 more than I was earning at Reading, and at that time it sounded like a fortune. I would have to move from my home town, but there was more than enough money to compensate for that.

I spoke to Maurice Evans, who had given me my big break, and I think he was a bit taken aback when I told him I wanted to sign for Gillingham. He asked me what they were offering and instructed me to join the rest of the players for training while he had discussions with the Reading chairman. By the time I'd showered and changed after the morning session I was called in to see Maurice and immediately offered a new contract that topped Gillingham by £20 per week. I was taken aback. At one stroke, Reading had effectively said they were willing to double my pay.

I had never wanted to leave Reading as the club had been good and Maurice had faith in me, but equally I didn't want to disappoint the Gillingham manager. I thought it would be a difficult conversation, telling Keith I would stay at Reading. But he was charming and said he understood, adding that he had always expected Reading to put up a fight to keep me.

It turned out to be a successful season for me personally, if not so for Reading. Following a good goal-scoring pre-season I scored in the opening Third Division game at Bradford City. It was a memorable goal for me, coming at the end of a long run from the halfway line.

I was scoring regularly and during the season Reading's local paper began reporting on how I was attracting the attention of West Bromwich Albion, Newcastle and Aston Villa. 'This season he looks ready to explode upon the Football League scene,' it reported 'He is the ideal build for a striker and looks stronger than at any previous stage in his career. There are still a few rough edges to his game which can certainly be smoothed out with expert coaching. It is his blistering pace which is the vital asset, and he makes most Third Division centre-backs look ponderous... If his promise is fulfilled he could well become as talented a centre-forward as any in the division and the club's saviour in more ways than one.' The article naturally gave me a lot of pleasure, and I learned from it that it was better for others to comment than for me to make boastful claims that could blow up in my face.

I scored four goals at Doncaster on 25 September 1982, but even so they won 7–5 and Reading slumped to twenty-second place in the table. My four goals got some coverage in the Fleet Street papers but I kept a low profile on purpose. Manchester United, Nottingham Forest, Arsenal and others were now being mentioned as clubs who were sending scouts to watch me. But it was Chelsea and Watford who were mentioned most frequently.

John Neal, the Chelsea manager, was a long-standing friend of Maurice Evans and he was frequently spotted at Elm Park, Reading's stadium in those days. Maurice was often quoted in the press saying I would make it big in the First Division, no doubt genuinely believing it, but also pushing up the price for Reading at the same time. To underline his point, I scored against First Division Watford in the quarter-finals of the Football League trophy in a 5–3 win, our fifth goal in extra time, pushing my tally up to twenty-three in twenty-five games.

The price probably went up again when Watford's own manager, Graham Taylor, was quoted as saying, 'Dixon is tremendous. Every time he got the ball he looked dangerous. He has applied like that every time I have seen him. How do they manage to keep hold of him?' Maurice claimed I was not for sale! Typical manager, pushing the price up, I'd have said. I was now top scorer in the entire Football League and a target for autograph hunters whenever we played away.

Fans called me 'Roy of the Rovers' – they had done so since I met Tom Tully, the writer of Roy Race's comic-strip adventures for three generations of Melchester Rovers followers. A story about Roy Race appeared in the programme alongside a picture of me and the fans latched onto it. It was a bit embarrassing when fans called out, 'Look, there's Roy of the Rovers.'

I was approached by two Reading-based journalists who offered to look after my business affairs and personal publicity now that my profile was beginning to rise. Brian Roach worked in the publicity department of the Rothmans cigarette company and Roger Ware worked with the *Daily Mirror*. They suggested starting a fan club and that I should make personal appearances, and I didn't see any harm in it. I met Brian's family, who were very nice, and he in turn met mine. He arranged for a newspaper column in the *Reading Evening Post* to appear under my name, for which I was paid a small fee. This was the first payment I had ever earned from football for activities outside the club.

Everything was going great until I slipped in some mud during a game just before Christmas and overstretched. The pitches were not what they are now, and we often lost our footing, even wearing long studs. Playing surfaces were dusty in the summer, when we wore rubber studs, and usually mud heaps in the winter. Today, pitches are like billiard tables, the boots are lighter, the ball is lighter, and you cannot tackle from behind or even the side. We were not afforded so much protection back then, and despite the injury I just got on with it and played another two games.

But I was stiffening up in these matches, and then I noticed a problem with the muscles in my groin. Soon I couldn't sit down at half-time or I wouldn't have been able to get up again. I knew that some people thought I was just being difficult, but that was ridiculous. The pain was so intense, that I couldn't train between games. Physio Glenn Hunter advised me to consult a Harley Street specialist. After numerous X-rays I was diagnosed with a pelvic problem and a Dr Nigel Harris advised rest for a month. I feared for my career as this was my first serious injury.

I had come so far. Now I even had my fan club, formed by Brian Roach with Kathy Taylor, who had finished third in the world modern pentathlon championships. She lived locally and became member No. 001. The fans raised my spirits at what was a difficult time. One, Margaret Bainbrigge, who had been a season ticket holder since the war, wrote me a lovely little poem while I was recuperating:

Kerry the striker, a brilliant lad
The best goal ace we've ever had
Quick on the turn, great in the air
And never a tackle that isn't fair
Here's wishing you well and a speedy return
To the game that you love and for which the fans yearn
So here's to you Kerry, keep your chin up
Who knows one day, you may win the cup.

I visited Margaret at her home in Tilehurst, near Reading, and thanked her personally. She told me she had been keeping a scrapbook of newspaper cuttings and photographs of my career and promised that when I played my first game for England she would present it to me – which indeed she did.

After a month I began talking to the team about risking a return to the pitch. We had about thirteen games left. Reading's plight was precarious and relegation loomed large. Before the injury I had set my sights on beating Ronnie Blackman's all-time goal-scoring record at Reading – thirty-nine league goals in 1951–2. With twenty-one goals in my first twenty-nine league games I had thought it possible, but the injury put paid to that.

Feeling optimistic about my recovery I kicked one of the training balls at our ground. The pain shot right through my body. It was back. I was dumbstruck. The following day I was due to travel to an important game at Cardiff to lend some moral support, and, luckily I felt better the next morning. On the coach to Cardiff, several of the lads were playing cards when another player, Ken Price, suddenly began to complain of a sore back. His condition worsened rapidly and the physio diagnosed muscle spasm. But there were only twelve players travelling, alongside coach Stewart Henderson. The simple solution was to switch someone into attack and promote Mark White from substitute, with the coach taking over as sub.

We stopped for the pre-match meal at a hotel by which time Ken was in desperate pain. I jokingly said I should make a comeback and everyone laughed. Yet, the idea stuck and I convinced myself I could do it – and convinced the manager too. Ken had a fitness test when we arrived but we all knew he had no chance. Maurice Evans came into the dressing room, looked long and hard at me, and said tersely, 'Get stripped.' I had to borrow one spare boot for my left foot from someone and another from someone else for my right, but I couldn't have been more overjoyed.

The Reading fans couldn't believe it either when I ran out; they went crazy. I'm convinced I'd have scored in the very first minute if I hadn't been barged in the back as I was lining up a header. But it brought a penalty, Stuart Beavon claimed the ball and missed. Still, we got a point from a goalless draw. I didn't have my usual zip, as the pain was still there, but I was sure I could play out the rest of the season.

I scored five in the final eleven games but I wasn't really myself. I captured the Golden Shoe for the division and yet I couldn't save Reading from the drop, despite scoring in the final game at Elm Park. The crowd were on the pitch, ready to celebrate, until a late goal from Exeter in their match at Newport put an end to our hopes.

This was the season in which publishing tycoon Robert Maxwell decided to try to merge Reading with his own club, Oxford United, to form a team called Thames Valley Royals, with a new stadium. The fight to save the club was led by former Reading player Roger Smee, by then a millionaire himself, and went all the way to the High Court before the merger was prevented. Brian Roach masterminded the counter-attack publicity campaign and later became a club director. But such was the uncertainty over our future that only Ken Price and I were signed up for the following season – and that was solely because we already had contracts. The new season had started before we knew we were going to be okay.

I received the Shoot/Adidas Golden Shoe in 1983 for being top scorer in the Third Division with twenty-six goals in thirty-five games, a total of fifty-one in one hundred and sixty games since signing from Dunstable. Interest in me as a player was growing as Roger Smee took over as chairman and slapped a £200,000 price on my head. Football writers from Fleet Street were calling all the time. I later discovered that Watford were keen to buy me once I had proved fully fit. In the end that didn't happen – much to Graham Taylor's regret, as I found out later. On England duty with John Barnes, we were staying in a room together when he took a call from Graham Taylor. Graham told him the biggest mistake he had ever made was not signing me when he had the chance.

The new chairman brought in Ian Branfoot from Southampton as first team coach and assistant to Maurice Evans, with Stewart Henderson demoted to the youth team. Ian was a hard task master, and pre-season was murder. He ran alongside me during a cross country run and said, 'You're Dixon aren't you?'

'Yes,' I replied.

'I've heard a lot about you,' came Ian's reply. I had the vibe that he didn't really rate me too highly.

Reading signed goal-scorer Trevor Senior from Portsmouth, sparking more gossip about my potential transfer. Unknown to me at the time, negotiations with Chelsea had reached an advanced stage. Then I heard that Reading had rejected a big offer from Stamford Bridge, which clearly disappointed me. Maurice told the press I was unusually loyal even though half the First Division clubs were chasing me. He said I was not banging on his door, agitating for a move, and I knew he would keep me in the picture,

Finally, I got the call I wanted. A deal with Chelsea had been agreed and I was to meet them for talks about terms. I was elated, but it didn't last long, for Roger then called to say the deal had broken down. They had agreed to pay £150,000, but my team wanted a promise of a further £25,000 if I ever made two or more appearances for England.

I was told to report to our Elm Park stadium the next morning for training as usual. I was disappointed, and felt as if I was all over the place.

The chairman called me the following morning at 8.00 a.m. 'You'll need an overnight bag,' he said. The deal was on again, and I was to report to Chelsea's pre-season training in Aberystwyth.

CHAPTER FOUR

STAMFORD BRIDGE

Chelsea chairman Ken Bates came to Elm Park himself to pick me up and drive me to Wales for pre-season training. I felt great excitement and anticipation about meeting him. In strode this chubby bloke with a pirate's beard; loud, abrasive, super-confident. Nothing like what I had expected.

We were introduced and, following a quick handshake, without any further pleasantries he snapped, 'Right, let's go.'

His Rolls-Royce was waiting outside. It was the first time I had ever been in one, let alone experienced the luxury of a Roller for a five-hour journey. I had a feeling it would be an interesting ride and I was not to be disappointed. The car was green with sumptuous leather seats and plush carpeting stretching up the side of the doors.

Ken and I talked about football and life in general and he very quickly eased my anxiety. I realised I was no longer in awe of him. In fact, I'd taken an instant liking to the man. I respected his attitude to life, and found his general demeanour appealing. To be perfectly frank, we got on like a house on fire.

Suddenly, he said, 'Right, we've had all the bullshit. How much do you want to sign for?'

I knew this was coming, although I expected it from manager John Neal and had taken advice from Maurice Evans on the kind of figure I could name. I hadn't a clue about the wages of First and Second Division players. Ken listened to what I had to say and went quiet for the first time since leaving Reading – but not for long.

He reeled off a list of names he could have signed for similar wages. He seemed to know the details of every single transfer in the game. Then he switched the conversation to how long I would play for them. Chelsea wanted me to sign a four-year agreement. I preferred two but, after a bit of wrangling, we compromised on three years. At no point did he make me feel uncomfortable or inferior, but I could see he was an extremely skilled and experienced negotiator. As quickly as the discussions had begun he brought them to an end, insisting the real talking would have to be done in consultation with the manager when we reached Aberystwyth.

He later revealed his own side of that first journey together, in the programme notes that accompanied my 1995 testimonial on leaving Chelsea. 'I picked him up from Reading to take him up to Aberystwyth where John Neal was taking pre-season training. I was under strict instructions not to discuss any possibility of a transfer. So for forty-five minutes we talked about everything under the sun. Then I said, "Do you want to join Chelsea or don't you?" We had a long conversation about it, got to Aberystwyth, he met the other guys, went to bed and went out training the next day. John "Holly" Hollins had just joined us as coach and he was a brilliant coach. We still hadn't discussed terms with Kerry, yet he was talking to Holly as "we".'

Batesy was proud and excited about his plans for what he continually termed 'the new Chelsea'. He explained to me exactly why he had stood by the manager when all believed he would be sacked following Chelsea's appalling performance in the Second Division the previous season. The club had finished fifth from the bottom, just two points away from relegation to the Third Division for the first time in their history.

My immediate impression of Bates was one of a man who enjoyed almost a perverse pleasure in proving other people wrong. He knew his own mind, and although he would consult with others he knew how to make his mind up. Sacking John Neal would have been the easy option, but Ken did things his way and he was astute enough to know that Chelsea's problem would not be cured by simply changing the manager.

He chatted excitedly and incessantly about the players who had already been signed during the summer of 1983; Joe McLaughlin, Pat Nevin, Eddie Niedzwiecki and Nigel Spackman, alongside John Hollins as player-coach. To be honest, while I knew Hollins after his hugely distinguished career and had played against Spackman, I hadn't a clue about the rest.

As we approached Aberystwyth I had the temerity to tell Batesy that one day I would like to have a Rolls-Royce to drive around in.

He replied, 'If you help to make Chelsea great again then you might get one. I intend to take this club to the top and if you do the job for which you will be handsomely paid you will grow with us.'

I was a bit unsure as to how I should address him. Should it be 'Mr Bates'? What about 'Mr Chairman'? The reply was typical of the man, 'Call me what you like, I don't care,' he said, 'Make it "Ken," if you want.' So, Ken it was – until Brian Roach heard me calling him Ken in conversation. He always made a point of calling him Mr Bates and was horrified by the way I had addressed the all-powerful owner of the club. I felt that he was one of the lads, down-to-earth, a normal fellow, a self-made man but Brian's observation troubled me. I had always been comfortable in Ken Bates' company but from that point I tried to avoid using his name at all.

Finally, I asked him straight out once more how I should address him. He replied with a grin, 'You've always called me Ken; carry on, I don't mind.' There it was, all agreed. From that moment on I called him 'Mr Chairman'.

As you may have realised, that Rolls-Royce journey made an indelible impression on me. In fact, Batesy (Mr Chairman) became a bit of a hero of mine, a man of achievement who became my example. I later visited his farm in Beaconsfield, just outside London, and that was fabulous and impressive too. Everything he did and owned was designed to astonish. I wanted that lifestyle.

That was the beginning of my relationship with one of the most colourful men in football. To this day I retain a healthy respect for the man. He was the Marmite of football as far as many were concerned, but I know how much he loved

Chelsea and how much he cared for the club – and still does – and what he did for it.. The fans have never lost sight of that, and they too hold him in high regard.

When we finally got to our destination in Wales, I was introduced to John Neal, the manager, his assistant Ian McNeill, and John Hollins, Peter Bonetti and Chelsea's youth development officer, Gwyn Williams. Ian had watched me many times – and many times had left disappointed – but he said he had spotted something I could do inside the box that made him think he needed to look again.

The players were staying in a hostel while the chairman was booked into a hotel. We all had dinner together and the chat was lively and the atmosphere particularly warm and friendly. John Neal was a quiet, deep-thinking character, proud of his no-nonsense Geordie origins. He didn't say too much at our first meeting and would answer me with a 'champion' or 'That's canny, aye.' With time I would realise that John was Batesy's Mr Fix-It, his go-to man, the great Chelsea survivor.

The two clubs had reached agreement on the size of the transfer fee but the real business of agreeing a suitable wage with me had yet to begin, despite the long chat in the Roller on the way up.

After dinner, the manager and the chairman slipped off for a quiet consultation before I was called over and discussions began in earnest. Bates left me to talk things over with John and I told him that, no matter what the outcome of our negotiations, I would want to discuss the entire matter with my parents before reaching any final decision on whether to sign. It was decided we'd leave it at that for the night and I was taken along to the youth hostel and given a room with instructions on the procedure for the following day.

All of the other players were in bed and I didn't see anyone until breakfast – at 8.30 a.m. sharp – the following morning. I walked into the dining room and sensed all the players examining the possible new boy. I sat down at the end of a long table and lads like Joe McLaughlin and Chris Hutchins went out of their way be friendly and welcoming. I was naturally a bit apprehensive because I didn't really know what to expect from training. I was very much aware that Chelsea wanted to see me in action before committing themselves because of my injury at the end of the previous season. I convinced myself I would be all right as I was experiencing no problem with the pelvic injury, and I had already completed ten days' pre-season training at Reading. The Chelsea boys had been at Aberystwyth for only two days so, I thought, I should have been in better shape than them. I had a rude awakening.

The manager believed that players should begin on sand, as it pulls at the muscles and drains the energy. My eagerness to impress soon proved to be my undoing. I should have known better. At Reading, we all took the mickey out of the apprentices because they never seemed to pace themselves. They'd fly around the opening lap of a race in about forty seconds and take a hundred more for the last. And just like an idiot, I charged into the first circuit around a sand dune while John Neal stood by, stopwatch in hand. It wouldn't have been so bad if I'd managed a great time for the lap, but it was only average. As soon as I stopped running my legs began to wobble and seize up. I collapsed in an untidy heap on the sand.

After a too-short breather, I had to pick up a baton and charge up a sand dune that slithered away under my feet. I somehow reached the summit, clawing at the sand, desperately fighting for some kind of hold. My head was spinning, my lungs were at bursting point and my legs were completely without feeling. How I managed to get over the top of that dune I will never know. I collapsed into a pathetic heap once more, fighting an overwhelming feeling of nausea. I honestly thought I was going to die. All of the lads were pointing at me and laughing hysterically. They thought it was wonderful to see their top-priced new boy struggling for his life. And if I'd been in their position I would have done exactly the same. What the hell was I doing?

Somehow I managed to do it all over again, my legs moving from memory. Then, just when I thought the agony was over, we were instructed to complete a run along the beach that stretched away over more than three miles. I'd always been hopeless at any kind of long-distance running and at Reading I would always be close to the back of the pack. Now I was against super-fit athletes, my legs still throbbing from the previous exercise, although at least we were allowed to walk to the start, detouring down to the sea to cool our feet and legs first. We were sent off to run in small groups.

I told winger Clive Walker that there was no chance of me making the finish, and he invited me to run alongside him, adding that he too was useless at any kind of distance running. I managed a mile but felt done for. It wasn't a question of running gently along the beach either, as there were rocks to be negotiated and breakwaters to jump. After time, I realised that I was holding Clive back, but he and a couple of others insisted on staying with me and somehow talked me through to the end.

Despite all the pain and agony I still wanted to sign for Chelsea. I liked the set-up, and the other players could see that I was no prima donna superstar strutting his stuff, but just an ordinary bloke.

When training ended, I was told the chairman wished to see me in his hotel in the early evening and after lunch some of the lads walked down to the town to watch *Superman III*.

During our meeting that evening, I was impressed again by Ken's attitude. He wanted the transfer sorted out quickly. Sheila Marson, the club secretary, arrived from London with the transfer and registration forms. This was moving too quickly – I had intended to discuss it all with my parents, with my agent and with Maurice Evans. Brian had called me earlier to say that other clubs were interested in matching the fee. Sheffield Wednesday and Watford headed the queue and Bobby Gould, manager of my dad's old club, Coventry, was flying back from his pre-season tour to talk to me.

I guessed that Batesy knew exactly what was going on – he never missed a trick – and he knew I wanted to go back to seek advice. He proposed an extremely fair offer, but he also made it quite clear that he had no intention of allowing me to leave without having signed for Chelsea. He warned me in no uncertain terms that if I left Aberystwyth and talked to the other clubs that the Chelsea offer would be withdrawn. Then he left me alone in his hotel bedroom to think things over.

When he returned he switched his powers of persuasion to full. He really sold the club to me; if he had his way, he said, I would sign immediately, have the medical the next day and turn out for Chelsea on the Saturday. I felt his ambition, that sense that something was going to happen, and I had seen the way that the passion for success jumped from him as chairman to the players. I found myself believing that there was every chance this club would be in the First Division very quickly – maybe even after just one season.

I made up my mind, but I wanted to speak with my dad first. Bates was curious. Why my dad? I said I consulted my parents about everything in my life. He invited me to talk to Dad right away. 'Speak to who the hell you like! Use the phone in this room, charge the calls to my account! But at the end of it all... I just want you to sign.'

I told my dad I liked the set-up, everything about it, and wanted to sign immediately. He asked if I was being put under pressure. I glanced at Batesy, sitting at the other end of the bed and over at Sheila Marson, waiting patiently at a desk in the room, the forms neatly laid out before her. No, no pressure! I managed to persuade Dad that it was all very relaxed.

Batesy later referred to this incident in the testimonial programme. 'An urgent message came from his father: some other team wanted to talk to him. He took the phone call and said, "I don't care, I want Chelsea." Sheila Marson drove up through the night with the forms and he signed next day. She drove back to register him. The rest is history.' I've no doubt that when the long-awaited Ken Bates autobiography finally appears we might learn much more about my signing and what else went on concerning me at the Bridge.

But he was right about one thing, I was keen to sign, so I would be better off not playing games with him. Perhaps he was bluffing when he threatened to withdraw the offer if I talked to other clubs, but I didn't want to take the chance. If anything, his tough talking sent him up in my estimation.

I put down the phone, walked over to Sheila and signed the forms.

I shook hands with Ken Bates.

'Welcome to Chelsea,' said the chairman. 'You won't regret the decision.'

Batesy had got what he wanted and I was sent back to London the following morning – this time in Sheila's Mini rather than the chairman's Roller!

I hadn't managed to speak to Maurice Evans before making the decision, but I retained great respect for him, and felt deep gratitude for what he did for me. There was no doubt he had an eye for a goal-scorer, having signed Trevor Senior to replace me. He also helped to sign John Aldridge and it was to be a shock when I heard that Reading sacked him after they went fourth in the table the following season. I sent a telegram of commiseration, followed by a letter of congratulations when he was appointed by Oxford United not long afterwards.

Back in London I faced a medical, and was worried about how the pelvic injury would look. Dr Millington, Chelsea's physician, was at Charing Cross Hospital to greet me and, after checking on my general condition, asked if I had sustained any serious injuries in my career. He took a number of X-rays and then left the room for what seemed like a considerable length of time. I began to fear the worst.

The injury was still there but, the doc eventually assured me, I was a fit and healthy young athlete. Was I still experiencing any pain from the pelvic area? I assured him there was no physical discomfort whatsoever.

He left the room again, this time to telephone Batesy in Aberystwyth. He returned much sooner this time and announced that the chairman and management were perfectly happy with my state of fitness, particularly after what they had seen for themselves in the training session. Thank goodness for those sand dunes, I thought.

Next day I returned to Reading – but as a Chelsea player. The lads were out training and I spoke to Roger Smee and thanked Maurice Evans for all he had done. I waited for my former teammates to finish training before saying goodbye.

I knew I had made the right decision. Chelsea were going places and I was going with them. I was already thinking of playing for England – but keeping it to myself.

Among my new fellow players was big, gangling centre-half named Joe McLaughlin, a bargain for Chelsea at just £90,000 from Greenock Morton thanks to Ian McNeill's expert knowledge of the Scottish market. Pat Nevin looked like a bit of a waif but was saluted as a genius reminiscent of Hughie Gallacher or Jimmy Johnstone. John Hollins was player-coach but could still play a bit, and had the enthusiasm of a nineteen-year-old.

There were six of us newcomers and while we were integrated with the likes of David Speedie, John Bumstead, Colin Pates and Colin Lee it was always clear that some in the old guard would have to make way. Resentment began to build up and the dressing-room banter could get fierce at times. Iconic figures such as Peter Osgood, Charlie Cooke and Alan Hudson had helped make Chelsea one of the most fashionable and glamorous clubs in the country back in the 1960s. Now it seemed to me that greats such as Hudson and the giant centre-half Mickey Droy were leading the faction that caused so much ill-feeling.

Hudson insisted on doing his own thing and playing his own way. He certainly didn't see eye to eye with the manager, coaching staff or the new contingent trying to transform the fortunes of the club. He always wanted to pick the ball up off the central defenders and pass it out to the full-back, and was only interested in playing in a deep position. The management were adamant that he should play much further forward, just behind the front two, where his extraordinary ability could be utilised in feeding the strikers and wingers.

Hudson's stubborn nature, his sheer bloody-mindedness, ensured he was not going to get on the team, which was a tragedy, but then much of his career could be described in similar terms; he was a rebel. Here was a player blessed with the kind of ability mere mortals like myself could only dream about and yet his attitude to the game in general, and to any kind of authority in particular, blighted a talent that should have been saluted as world-class.

Even when he was finally squeezed out at Stamford Bridge his sniping continued with distasteful newspaper articles in which he slagged off players he'd left behind. Perhaps he needed the money badly, but I was one of his targets and he told the world that in his opinion I couldn't play. There are some people in the game who would have upset me deeply if they'd come out with a similar appraisal, but Hudson's words and opinions had long since ceased to count for anything.

More practically, Hudson and a few others threatened to destroy any semblance of team spirit. Droy was also not picked for the team now being hailed as the 'new Chelsea'.

The two of them would watch the first half at the Bridge and, if it wasn't going well, they'd disappear into the players' bar for the rest of the game, where they'd pass derogatory comments about those who had taken their places. John Neal knew he had to get them out of the club. Relationships were so strained between old and new that I was thankful I had five other new signings to share the flak with.

David Speedie told me it had been a nightmare for him since being signed from Darlington some time earlier. He couldn't seem to do anything right for the old guard and he had almost reached the point of desperation. Fortunately, Speedo is made of sterner stuff. He was helped by a quiet word from John Neal, who said the situation was going to change rapidly. John knew he had the backing of the chairman and that he and a handful of other decent lads and honest professionals would stay, while the rest would be sold off. Speedo and I were to discover that John Neal was a man who lived up to his promises.

We didn't see much of Ken Bates when I first arrived – he seemed to be on the news more often than he was with us – but there were a couple of occasions on which he came into the dressing room and laid down the law. This was to be a new era, he said, and any player, whether recently signed or on the team for years, would be thrown out if he didn't pull his weight in the common cause. Ken was a chairman who demanded strong discipline and high standards.

The squad's new backbone took the form of Eddie Niedzwiecki in goal, Joe McLaughlin at centre-back and me at centre-forward. Surprisingly, Speedo, with whom I was to later form an effective partnership, played below standard in pre-season games and was left out of the opening matches while I partnered Colin Lee up front.

I scored my first goal in a friendly at Wimbledon in a 2–1 defeat, but I only properly entered the big time on 29 August 1981, with my Chelsea debut against Derby County.

CHAPTER FIVE

HIGHS AND LOWS AT THE BRIDGE

It was a debut dream for me when we played Derby County. Magnificent! The new Chelsea were off and running as we trounced them 5–0, the biggest win of the day in the entire Football League.

Derby's manager, Peter Taylor, admitted that his side were humiliated. I made one goal for Clive Walker and smacked in two of my own, the first a very satisfying half-volley (one headline read 'KERRY GOLD!' That one stuck).

The following day, We were not mentioned in the press in terms of our possibly being promoted at a time when all the talk about promotion favourites centred on Newcastle United inspired by Kevin Keegan, Sheffield Wednesday and Manchester City. No one said anything in our dressing room after the game, but we all felt it. We knew it was a possibility.

We beat Gillingham in the first leg of the Milk Cup first

round. I put Clive through for an equaliser and scored the winner with a header and soon I was being compared to Chelsea legend Peter Osgood. I'd never seen Ossie play, except on TV, but I would have settled for matching his achievements.

Two more goals in a 2–1 win at Brighton and the fans had taken to my style. Inevitably, we had a couple of setbacks, but we did manage a 4–0 win over Gillingham when I scored all four. A total of nine in my first six games – it was a great feeling to have hit the ground running. As a striker I always needed to get goals. Winning is important for the team, but for a striker its all about goals. Don't listen to what we tell you when we are interviewed – 'Oh, yes, it didn't matter that I scored so long as the team won.' That's true – everyone plays their part in the team, but my part was to score.

It's an attitude that can be taken to extremes, however. I have heard it said by certain scorers that they would rather lose 4–1 as long as it's they who get the one goal. I won't name names but it's the wrong way to go about it. Yet it is a basic truth. Defenders want clean sheets, strikers want goals.

Soon I was being hailed as the new Malcolm Macdonald. I liked that as Super Mac had been a favourite of mine when I stood on the terraces at Luton marvelling at his incredible speed and deadly finishes.

By now Chelsea were hovering around the top two, but it wasn't all sweetness and light – far from it. I didn't like David Speedie, for a start. On the field we became one of the most feared partnerships in the game. He was good at all the things I wasn't so good at, and the same was true the other way around. We quickly developed a telepathy. I knew if he was going to get to the ball to head it on – for a small man he could jump all right, and he had great ability. You can include Pat Nevin as part of the set-up, as well. He created some great chances for us both with some terrific wing play and trickery. I had a tremendous admiration for Speedo's fierce commitment and drive, and the outstanding energy of the little fellow never ceased to amaze me.

But, for a start, he didn't command a regular place in the team. Instead, his closest pal, Colin Lee, was selected to partner me. Speedo made it quite clear he thought he should be in the team which was fair enough. But I became the target of his moaning, groaning and general displeasure when it would have made more sense for him to be annoyed at his mate, Colin, for being in the team. I sensed a genuine animosity toward me. Speedo was jealous that I had signed for a big fee and was grabbing the glory with the goals. This feeling was not just over-sensitivity on my part. Colin Lee had played in the First Division for Spurs while I was just a country boy from the sticks who had come up from way down the lower leagues.

Yet even when Speedo won a place in the team there was no let-up. If I failed to control a ball in training he'd laugh in a derisory way, or raise his eyebrows in a kind of mock horror. Maybe it was because I was the new boy that I didn't bite back at first, but a major confrontation was inevitable. And it came following a defeat at the Bridge on 3 December 1983 to Manchester City, one of our great rivals for promotion.

I'd been happy with my form, having scored eleven goals in seventeen league games, plus cup goals before the fateful encounter. Two goals from me and one from Paul Canoville had smashed Huddersfield's unbeaten home record of thirty-three games, and I had another brace next up beating Fulham

5–3 at Craven Cottage, as well as a goal at Leeds with a draw that pushed us into second for the first time in the season.

There was a big buzz at the Bridge on 3 December with a crowd of almost 30,000, but behind the scenes the atmosphere was not so warm. Speedo and Lee had been having a go at me in training throughout the previous week. I knew that if I made even the slightest mistake in the game they'd throw their hands up in exasperation and glare at me as though I was some kind of imbecile, and I had warned Joe McLaughlin, my closest pal, that if there were any more derogatory comments from Speedo I was going to hit him.

The team was not playing well that night and we were a goal behind. Speedo started up front with me and Lee was introduced from the bench in place of Peter Rhodes-Brown to form a three-pronged attack. One of my great assets and strengths as a goal-scorer is an uncanny sixth sense about where the ball will drop in a crowded penalty area. It was from that attacking set-up that the bad feeling between Speedo and Lee and me came to a head. Lee urged me to make a run towards the near post as a cross was about to come in. I ignored him because I was expecting the ball to be played into the crowded goal-mouth. The cross was played to the far post and the chance of an equaliser disappeared. Lee and Speedo began their sniping. I warned Speedo that if he opened his mouth again I'd put my fist in it.

He looked shocked and muttered something like, 'Oh, you just do your own thing then.'

With about five minutes of the game left my anger was rising. Back in the dressing room I challenged him, 'Have you got anything else to say?' I demanded.

'Oh, shut up,' he said. I saw red and punched him in the face. He tried to retaliate but other players rushed in between us and kept us apart.

'Right,' I shouted. 'We'll finish this later.'

No serious damage done, but the manager was not at all pleased and ordered us to report to his office as soon as we had changed.

I felt empty inside. After weeks of pent-up emotion it was all out in the open. My temper had not subsided by the time Speedo and I were in the manager's office where I told John Neal that I was not prepared to endure the situation a moment longer. He sat behind his desk quietly contemplating my rage. I told him there would be a written transfer request on his desk by Monday morning. I was no longer prepared to stay with a club where I was being slaughtered by teammates intent on taking the mickey at every available opportunity.

'I'm finished with this club. I want away.'

Speedo was silent for once. Finally, he said, 'People can't say anything to you but it's okay for you.'

Ever since I had joined Chelsea he had made my life a misery. It should have been a time of joy with the number of goals I was scoring. I told him all that. Again, he was silent. I looked at him, and my anger drained away. It's impossible to explain exactly why, but I began to feel sorry for him. I felt enlightened, as if I was beginning to understand his motives. Perhaps his own great desire to be a success had overwhelmed him. He looked genuinely upset and disturbed by what had happened, and on reflection I saw that I had reacted badly. Joe insisted later I had been right to strike out, but in that moment in John Neal's office I knew it was out of order. Silly, emotional stuff, and two responsible men should have known better.

John ordered me to report to his office on Monday morning while Speedo was instructed to stay behind that night. I don't know what was said to him after I left the ground. I returned home and related the incident to my dad. He told me to forget the idea of a transfer for the moment, although he accepted that the situation could not be allowed to continue. He advised me to let the manager sort things out and we would talk about the next move only if John Neal was unable to do so. I was happy enough to forget about the transfer threat because it had been made in the heat of the moment. When I reported to the ground on Monday morning no one mentioned the incident and, after saying 'good morning' to everyone I went out to do my training. I have never been the type to bear a grudge and thankfully the matter was closed.

It soon seemed that the clash was the best thing that could have happened to Speedo and me, as our relationship, both personally and professionally, blossomed from that point onward. Maybe the outburst allowed each of us to understand the other's temperament much more than we had. He certainly seemed to realise I was every bit as competitive as he was, and I came to admire his gutsy, passionate approach. He was still a moaner, but, I realised, certainly no more so than I was. We continued to earn our outstanding reputation as a partnership, and although we continued to criticise each other, the tone was different. We kept each other on our toes and off the pitch and I came to like him as a man very much indeed.

I wasn't the only player who came to blows with Speedo at one time or another, but I'd say all these arguments were just part of the thread that Chelsea wove into the fine team it was becoming. The players knew that this might be their only chance of success and they were determined to take it. Speedo was no different; he'd been signed from the lower divisions and had no intention of going back. Our altercations were born out of pride and ambition and the manager must have been secretly delighted by the new team, particularly after the nightmares of the previous season that had almost cost him his job.

The spirit within the camp grew until there was a warm feeling of complete togetherness. The moans and groans gave way to encouragement and positivity. We were determined to get out of the Second Division. In the very next match following my bust-up with Speedo we thrashed Swansea 6–1 at the Bridge with a Paul Canoville hat-trick. We were becoming an irresistible force, our confidence boosted by a Milk Cup second round triumph over First Division Leicester, although we went out in the next round to West Brom. Sheffield Wednesday had been top all season but we began to press them hard

Portsmouth at the Bridge was a game to remember. It was just after Christmas and Mark Hateley, one of my rivals for a place in the England team, opened the scoring and Paul Canoville equalised. I was back helping the defence when I handled and Pompey scored from the penalty. A couple of minutes later Speedo was brought down. I'd scored from the spot in the previous two games but not this time, as Alan Knight saved my penalty brilliantly. I scored an equaliser with seven minutes left of the first half. Speedo was brought down again and we got a second penalty. I changed direction and beat the keeper, but the ball struck the bar and the match ended in a draw.

Despite my penalty performance, John Neal insisted that if we got another in our next game he would still want me to take it. Our next game was at Brighton on New Year's Eve, and sure enough there was another penalty. I thought, Oh, no, not again. The team were split – should I or shouldn't I? I was not going to chicken out. However, it happened yet again. Joe Corrigan pulled off a great save. A big groan went up from the fans who had only seconds earlier been giving me so much encouragement. Speedo scored the winner with just eleven minutes left – that cheered me up a little. The win took us to the top of the table for the first time that season.

I made a vow to myself, there and then – no more penalties; but, to be honest, it was a case of my quitting before I was sacked.

Management had decided we would leave Brighton for the north-east that day in order to prepare for our game with Middlesbrough on 2 January 1984. We were not happy but they were clearly concerned we might overdo the New Year celebrations. It was quite a trip from Brighton to Middlesbrough, but we were promised a hot meal when we got to the hotel.

Sandwiches and a few sad looking lettuce leaves greeted us on our arrival, and noticeably failed to lighten the mood. John Hollins had a word with management and we went out for meal. John Neal said we could see the New Year in as long as we were in bed shortly after midnight. But after a few drinks no one was in the mood for an early night, particularly as we had a day to recover before the match. It was not to be, however. John ushered us up to our rooms as soon as the last chime faded. We pleaded for extra time – a few of us were tipsy enough to think it would be amusing to hide and he became increasingly annoyed. Even so, by 1.00 a.m. all of us were finally in our beds and well on the way to sleeping soundly but we still got a major rollicking the next morning. I don't think I had ever seen John so angry. The lecture just made us all the more determined to do well for him.

We didn't. We failed miserably. It was a filthy day, raining incessantly and the pitch was an absolute quagmire. I missed an open goal right at the start and most of the lads were well below par. We were a goal down at half-time until Tony McAndrew – who had previously been with Boro when John Neal was manager – equalised. But then Eddie Niedzwiecki slipped as he was drop-kicking from the goal, allowing the ball to slither to the edge of the penalty area where David Currie picked it up and went around Eddie to score the winner.

There was a deathly silence in our dressing room after the game. As players, we were convinced that the celebrations of New Year's Eve had nothing to do with our lacklustre performance, but it was immediately evident that the management did not agree. John Neal was fuming, Ian was speechless and Hollins had a real go at the players.

It was a long journey home. We knew if we were to gain promotion we had to win games like this and we had let ourselves down badly. And the situation only got worse that weekend with a 1–0 defeat in the third round of the FA Cup at Blackburn Rovers.

John Neal made it clear to us all that he was not prepared to stand by and risk the distinct possibility of squandering an outstanding opportunity to return to the First Division. His solution was to buy Welsh international Mickey Thomas – an inspired move. He knew all about Thomas because he had brought him into the game when he was manager at Wrexham. Thomas proved good for the club not only because of his talent, but also for his extrovert personality. Both he and his Welsh national teammate Joey Jones had an impish sense of humour and they were great for team spirit, lifting everybody's morale.

A 2–1 win at Derby, with Tony McAndrew scoring the winner from a penalty, set us up for the highlight of the season, a home game with Sheffield Wednesday in front of more than 35,000 fans. We stormed into a two-goal lead by half-time, Mickey scoring both, and a third from Pat Nevin gave us a 3–2 victory to go top of the Second Division.

Two more from me and one from Speedo saw off Huddersfield in the next match in February, we beat Cambridge, drew at home to Carlisle – costing us the top spot – but we were back on top after goals from myself, Speedo and a penalty for Tony meant we beat Oldham 3–0. The team continued to play with tremendous confidence at the top of the table. We went three down at Cardiff but I scored in the second half, which along with a goal from Nigel Spackman and a penalty for Colin Lee, earned us a point for a draw. I scored two more against Fulham in a 4–0 win.

Our chance to seal our promotion came on a warm, sunny afternoon at the Bridge on 7 April, against Leeds United. I scored two in the first half and one eight minutes into the second, following on from Mickey Thomas, who had begun the goal rout back in the fifth minute of the game.

A ring of policeman held back the jubilant fans just yards from the pitch. A minute from time Paul Canoville, who had come on as sub, scored a glorious fifth and the crowd poured onto the pitch. The ref was knocked over in the rush and the worry was that the match would be called off at this late stage. But he recovered after treatment and insisted the incident had been a pure accident. He understood fully the excitement and exuberance of our supporters, who, fortunately, responded to an appeal over the loudspeaker system to vacate the area. But he knew the Chelsea players would be mobbed as soon as the final whistle sounded.

Well aware of what was about to happen, the ref awarded a free kick and then whispered to the players that he was about to end the game. We began to edge our way towards the safety of the players' exit, and when the final whistle blew managed to escape unscathed. Good thinking by the referee – the most sensible match official I'd come across. The supporters massed on the pitch and we joined in their celebration of our promotion to the First Division from the safety of the directors' box. It was incredible to think that we had been 25–1 outsiders at the start of the season to win promotion.

The crushing 5–0 defeat sent Leeds down to twelfth place and in their fury, their fans smashed our electric scoreboard in fury. Bricks and masonry were hurled at policemen, although the incident was quickly subdued.

The next job was winning the Second Division title. We first had to play Manchester City, whose own promotion push had faded, in a game that was to be televised live. All the talk was of the new, vibrant young Chelsea team about to take on the First Division. My goal that day was the epitome of the splendid team play that had become our hallmark in the second half of the season. Paul Canoville combined with Speedo and then I headed in the cross to score what became one of the contenders for Goal of the Season. Pat Nevin provided the second.

A home win over Barnsley set up the championship decider in the last game of the season. Victory at Grimsby on 12 May would give us the title. So many Chelsea fans wanted to see this game that the section of the ground allocated to them couldn't contain them and they spilled over the barriers, gasping for air. The referee took the players off the field and back to the dressing room and the game was suspended for fifteen minutes, meaning Sheffield Wednesday against Cardiff at Ninian Park would finish well before our match.

After coming close a couple of times I scored with a header from Pat's cross. Speedo was brought down but this time I wasn't looking to take the penalty and the keeper made a great save of Pat's attempt. News filtered through that Sheffield had won 2–0, but our defence held out. We were going back to the First Division as champions. We were euphoric – and celebrated with a few beers on the way back.

I'd scored thirty-four goals, the best in the division, twenty-eight of them in the League and six in the Milk Cup. And I also missed three penalties! We had not lost a single League game since we let ourselves down at Middlesbrough. We had won thirteen of the last seventeen games, drawing four, in the most eventual season of my career so far.

The mood was so buoyant and light-hearted that even Batesy joined in the festivities. We had hatched a secret plan to throw the chairman in the team bath. Well, not so secret, as it turned out. He always seemed to know everything going on in the League and this was no exception. He strolled into the dressing room, calm as you please and said, 'Okay, boys, I'll go quietly.' With that he jumped, fully clothed, into the bath and sat there among the boys in his suit with water dripping off his spectacles. He was clearly a good sport and a lot more human than the media painted him. To me he was not so much an ogre as a mischievous old rascal.

Now he was sitting beside me, and as ever he knew when to take part, just as he knew when to leave managers to manage. He had every reason to celebrate – he had taken over a club on the brink of bankruptcy and turned it around.

John Neal had gone even further in taking us to the First Division. Just how far we only learned later that summer. I was shocked when I heard he had undergone emergency open-heart surgery; a life or death procedure involving four separate by-passes in a five-hour operation. The arteries around his heart were 95 per cent useless and a massive heart attack was imminent. He was a keen smoker and apparently had one last fag before surgery. Fortunately, he made a quick recovery.

He hadn't told us the full extent of his problems, but I had suspected for some time that his health was not as sound as it might be. There were times toward the end of the season when he abandoned his bench in the final stages of vital matches. I think I knew that he was a sick man but I don't think it was an exaggeration to say that he had almost killed himself with the effort of restoring Chelsea to the First Division. I remember that in the last fifteen minutes of the final game at Grimsby he hadn't been able to stand up at all and eventually returned to the dressing room. But his passion for the game ran as deep as that of anyone I knew. I was reminded of Bill Shankly's famous comment, 'Some people believe football is a matter of life and death... I can assure you it is much, much more important than that.'

CHAPTER SIX

BACK IN THE FIRST DIVISION

Another pre-season training spent slogging up and down the dreaded sand dunes of Aberystwyth got me fit, and I was already excited by my debut in the First Division. It was August 1984, Chelsea were back in the top flight after seven years, playing Arsenal on a warm, sunny morning. We received a great welcome from the Chelsea fans at Highbury; there must have been 20,000 there.

Doug Rougvie, a big rugged Scot, was one of the summer signings, a full-back from Aberdeen. He soon made his presence known when Arsenal right-back Viv Anderson over-ran the ball slightly coming down the right. The new man went into the tackle so hard that Viv went about six feet up in the air and over the top of Doug.

Paul Mariner headed the Gunners in front from a Kenny Sansom free kick, but four minutes later came the most exciting moment of my career so far. Doug put over a free kick, I latched onto the ball as it bounced in the penalty area, hit it first time with my left foot, the shot rebounded off the legs of Pat Jennings and looped in the air. I recovered a split-second faster than the defenders and volleyed the rebound with my right foot. I had emulated my dad and scored in the First Division in a game that ended in a draw.

I spoke to Dad, as I did after every game and he didn't say anything different about my debut goal in the First Division – just the usual 'Well done.' He was always straight to the point, and he would also look at the things I didn't do well. I appreciated his sound advice and anyway, I knew he was thrilled to bits, as indeed was my mum.

I didn't have time to dwell on the start of the season as I immediately began thinking about the next game that was coming up on Tuesday. I liked playing midweek much more than training, and there was always an extra day off. There was no time to pause. Today's footballers, by contrast, earning a hundred times what I did, are always moaning about needing to rest and playing too many games. I've never heard so much crap in my life. I think they have it a damn sight easier than the generation before them. They have massages before and after each game, when we were lucky to find a shower that worked on our away trips.

We played Friday night live on TV against Everton, who had won the FA Cup the previous season. I remember that Batesy was against entire matches live on TV, convinced it would kill the game although, of course, he changed his tune later on!

As it turned out, the live TV offering was a bit of a damp squib. I hit the bar but also missed a couple of other chances and, while it seemed like it would be a goalless draw, they nicked a late winner. We were all deeply disappointed at suffering our first defeat in the First Division with the entire nation watching. But we were up against a good team. Everton marched on to win the League and the European Cup Winners' Cup that season.

I hadn't scored since the start of the season and didn't in our next match. I started to become a touch concerned as the media hiked up the pressure on me. John Neal was still recuperating, leaving Ian McNeill and John Hollins in charge, although none of the players ever quite knew which one was picking the team.

Whoever it was who was in charge kept faith with me and I started the next game against Aston Villa. But we crashed to a 4–2 defeat in which, for the first time in my career, I was pulled off. I was devastated when I saw the number '9' held up on the touchline. I went straight to the dressing room and sat alone in the team bath. I was bitterly disappointed and felt as though I was at a crossroads in my career. I wondered whether I could make it at this level.

My anxious state of mind was not improved when I saw reserve centre-forward Derek Johnstone report for training the following morning with the rest of the first team squad of thirteen. I was convinced he was there with a view to taking my place. The reserves had played a game the previous night in which he'd scored.

My anger prevented me from concentrating on the training session and afterwards I went to see Hollins and demanded to know what was going on. 'If I am about to be dropped you should tell me to my face.'

He replied calmly, 'What gave you that idea?' He didn't wait for a response. 'As far as I am concerned you stay in the team to play yourself out of the bad patch.' Without any prompting, Johnstone had simply volunteered to come in for extra training. But I didn't like it. I still suspected Johnstone was up to something. He'd read the papers – and I was beginning to think the press were part of a campaign to get rid of me – and knew I'd been pulled off at Villa, and I was sure he was out to stake his claim. I was depressed enough as it was, I thought, and I didn't need this.

My dark thoughts just showed my insecurity, particularly as Hollins was as good as his word and I stayed in the team. Johnstone didn't report for extra shift work again. I began to recover my form, responding well against West Ham by making a goal for Speedo in a 3-0 win. Hollins further boosted my confidence by telling me and then the media that I had played well. But I knew I still needed a goal.

John Neal soothed my anxieties when he looked in at the ground and offered his usual sound advice. I wasn't to worry and was simply to concentrate on playing my normal game. He had always been a great believer in simplicity and he knew that if I stuck to what I did best the goals would flow again. He assured me he was still the manager and that I would always be in his team. Hollins and Neal were also helpful as I worked through this period of crisis.

Playing Luton Town at Kenilworth Road seemed the ideal moment to end my goal drought, but it didn't happen . A disappointing goalless draw prompted headlines such as DIXON'S HEAD ON THE BLOCK.

When the tide eventually turned it was in a Milk Cup

second-round, first-leg tie at the Bridge against Millwall. First I played a ball through for Speedo that was turned into an own goal. Then, a minute later, at long last, came my first goal in seven games, and a beauty, even if I say so myself. A huge burden had been lifted off my shoulders. I got a second, and all was well with the world again.

Next game against Leicester at the Bridge at the end of September I got the first two in a 3-0 win. Two followed later against Watford, although that didn't prevent John Barnes scoring a brilliant winner.

The team's fortunes didn't look so good after a 1–0 defeat at Southampton when we went down to seventeenth place. However, I got both goals in a 2–0 win over Ipswich and I was particularly pleased as I was up against a player I rated highly, England centre-half Terry Butcher.

At home I played my first game against my dad's old club, Coventry, in November, although it didn't go according to plan, at least not to begin with. Coventry went two up, but I pulled one back when we equalised and then we ran amok. I headed my second from Pat Nevin's cross. The electric scoreboard lit up: 'Come on Kerry, you're not going home until you get your hat-trick.' With ten minutes left I obliged – my debut First Division hat-trick. We finished up with one more, literally hitting them for six.

By now, I was the leading scorer in the First Division, with ten from thirteen games. So much for all my negative thoughts.

David Speedie wasn't doing so well. He was struggling for goals at a time when the club had bought another recognised goal-scorer in the form of Gordon Davies from Fulham, who had watched the game from the stands. The papers were claiming that the new boy was a replacement for Speedo and Gordon didn't help himself in – quite innocently – choosing Speedo's usual spot in the dressing room for his very first training session. Speedo said in mock outrage, 'Not only are you after my place in the team, you've already pinched my peg!' He joined in the laughter, but I knew it must have disguised the sort of anxieties I had recently been harbouring about my own place in the team. But John Hollins had some encouraging words in the press for Speedo, too. It was made clear that the new signing was tasked with working alongside Pat Nevin to create openings for me.

The goals continued to flow, and I got my second hat-trick in a 4–1 Milk Cup win over Manchester City that put us in the quarter-finals. There was even speculation that I would be called up by England until Bobby Robson named some sixty players for three internationals and I was not one of them. But I was becoming increasingly well-known. Billy McNeill, who had been managing Manchester City for the past year, said he hadn't heard of me during his time in Scotland in charge of Celtic, but now he thought I was the best centre-forward in England. I got 'footballer of the month' in both the *Daily Mirror* and in London's *Evening Standard*.

Rightly, John Hollins sounded a note of caution, warning me not let the publicity go to my head. But he didn't need to say it. I was focused only on improving my game until I could fulfil my burning ambition to be picked for England.

I scored against Liverpool in December, following a tackle on Alan Hansen. Perhaps I shouldn't have bothered – I wasn't known for my challenges and usually left it to Speedo who was more tenacious, to say the least. I managed to damage my knee ligaments in the process and I could tell the moment it happened that the injury was something fairly serious. That wasn't the only bit of bad news. Speedo was booked in the game and that meant there was an all-new strike-force the following week, with Derek Johnstone finally getting his big chance as the team earned a creditable draw against Sheffield Wednesday. Gordon Davies scored on his debut. After two weeks, I returned to play against Stoke and scored, but hadn't fully recovered.

In the Boxing Day game with QPR I broke my vow not to take any more penalties. I didn't need much encouragement as to me it was nothing more than another opportunity to score a goal. This time I was successful and I pulled it off again in the same game following another penalty. The jinx had well and truly been broken.

I had another barren spell, but towards the end of January 1985, in the FA Cup third round replay at Wigan, I made my FA Cup scoring debut with not just one but four goals. We won 5-0 and even the Wigan manager was heard praising me after the match. John Neal, still in recovery from his operation, said that Bobby Robson was going to have no choice but to pick me.

I missed another penalty against Sheffield Wednesday in the Milk Cup at the Bridge, forcing us into an unwanted replay. We were three down by half-time when the dressing room talk was all about damage limitation and playing for pride. But then I played a part in Paul Canoville getting one, before I scored our second myself. Mickey Thomas smashed in the equaliser and Paul Canoville put us in front with five minutes to go after I crossed from the right. Unfortunately, they scored a late penalty and there were no more goals in extra time.

We won the replay to set up a two-legged semi-final against Sunderland, but it didn't go well. We lost our centre-half early on with a dislocated shoulder, Colin Lee was soon no more than a passenger after damaging a hamstring, and Mickey Thomas had a rib injury. Young Dale Jasper replaced Joe, handled and conceded a penalty and although Eddie saved it, West scored on the rebound. We felt we could pull back the two goals in the second leg especially when Speedo scored early. Clive Walker, who had been at Chelsea when I first joined, scored a glorious goal and he scored again as we pushed to get back into it; we lost 5–2 on aggregate.

Seven goals in the last thirteen games meant that I ended my First Division season as joint leading scorer on twenty-four with Gary Lineker, who was then at Leicester. I'd also scored eight goals in the Milk Cup and four in the FA Cup to make a total of thiry-six. For the third season in a row I won the Adidas Golden Boot, the first player ever to win the award over three divisions.

Surely now I had convinced Bobby Robson?

CHAPTER SEVEN

ENGLAND IN THE AZTECA

I was haunted by the countless number of times Bobby Robson had been in the stands watching me. It began to affect my performance. I always seemed to have a poor game when he turned up but I was so desperate to impress him. He might have begun to realise that himself, commenting, 'Maybe it is a good job I haven't seen every game Kerry's played this season otherwise he might have scored only seven rather than thirty-six goals.'

It was rumoured that the England manager liked my goal-scoring ability but not my touch. Or it was my technique he didn't rate. It was tough to sift fact from fiction. One journalist wrote that the England manager shouldn't worry about my first touch as my last touch was devastating – now, that I liked.

The media got wind of the fact that I also qualified to play for Ireland and Wales. Although I was born in Luton, both my parents came from Ireland, while my grandfather on my mother's side had been born in Wales. That made no difference to me – I only wanted to play for England.

I wonder if the game against Anfield in May 1985 changed Bobby Robson's opinion of me? We had come back from 3–1 down against Liverpool only to lose 4–3, but I'd scored and was well pleased with my performance (if not the result). Liverpool keeper Bruce Grobbelaar said it was 'silly' that I wasn't in the England team. And – whatever the reason – within a fortnight I was in the line-up.

It had been a tense couple of weeks. The England squad was going to Finland for an important World Cup qualifier, followed by a friendly with Scotland and then a summer tournament in Mexico and the USA. Everyone wanted to know who would be playing. Just as I'd hoped, Robson said that the number of goals I'd racked up had made me impossible to ignore. He also felt that I lacked finesse – but then, the same thing had been said about Gerd Müller. I still had to pinch myself when John Hollins took me aside during training to give me the news. Robson had reasoned that the only way to discover if I could produce goals at international level was to give me a chance to do it. I'm not much given to outbursts of emotion, but inside I was buzzing. I didn't go around telling everyone apart from giving the good news to my parents on the phone. But word got around, and the Chelsea lads congratulated me the next day.

I was pretty apprehensive, as you would expect, to be joining the elite of English football. I need not have been concerned. We met at the airport hotel the night before the trip at the end of May and the lads in the squad were warm and friendly. Chris Waddle, Terry Butcher and Kenny Sansom were particularly welcoming.

At the airport Bobby Robson pulled me to one side, congratulating me on my selection. He asked if I would mind playing for the Under-21 team against Finland on the night before the big World Cup qualifier. He explained he was short of strikers for the game and I could qualify as an over-age player under the rules of the competition. In any case, he was not intending to play me in the main game because it was important I should settle down as a member of the squad and Mark Hateley was his number one centre-forward. I would have agreed to anything – I was just dead keen to be wearing an England shirt for the first time in my life. That was more than enough for me.

I got on the first rung of the international ladder playing a game alongside great players such as Stewart Robson of Arsenal and West Ham's Tony Cottee. The match was played in a remote town and after only seventeen minutes we were two down. But the moment I had been waiting for arrived in the second half when I volleyed a shot into the corner of the net, although it didn't stop Finland getting their first-ever victory over England with a 3–1 win. At least Dave Sexton, in charge of the Under-21s, told me he thought I had done well in my first representative game, and had taken my goal splendidly.

I watched the World Cup qualifier the next day from the stands, feeling very much part of the squad and I was much encouraged and looking forward to the Scotland-England game at Hampden Park and the summer tour. My main rival for the No. 9 jersey, Mark Hateley, got the goal in a creditable 1–1 draw, and I cheered as much as anyone. His score put us one step closer to qualification.

The England party flew to Troon to prepare for the Scotland game, for which I was named one of the subs. I got as far as being instructed to warm up, but when Glenn Hoddle came off it was Trevor Francis who went on and the Scots won with a fine header from Richard Gough.

We were allowed to return home to our families for just a couple of days before reporting for the long journey to Mexico City for the 1985 pre-World Cup tour, for the main competition was to be held in Mexico the following year. Bobby Robson told us that we would all be at least one game as the Italy-based players – Mark Hateley, Ray Wilkins and Trevor Francis – were scheduled to return to their clubs after the second game to play in the Italian Cup.

The first training session in the heat and altitude of Mexico was something else. Even a gentle jog up the stairs at the hotel was an effort, and during vigorous exercise, breathing was particularly hard. My throat felt so constricted that I had to fight for every gasp of air. The 600-metre training sprints were killers, and after each burst England doctor Vernon Edwards and the coaching staff would check our pulses to measure the recovery rate. We finished up with an exhausting twelve minute run. Gary Stevens proved to be a natural athlete, and he led the field with Bryan Robson, Dave Watson and John Barnes. I was surprised and delighted to have finished in the middle of the pack – much better than I thought I would do. Throughout training we underwent blood and urine tests, our body weight was checked constantly and our food intake carefully monitored and supplemented with iron and salt tablets.

We all went to watch world champions Italy play World Cup hosts Mexico in the magnificent Azteca stadium – although its appearance was deceptive. We later found out for ourselves that it wasn't so cosy inside the dressing rooms, which tended to be constantly flooded. The Italians had been in Mexico for some time doing thorough preparation, as you'd expect. They had already played a couple of warm-up games against club sides and looked good to me, and fully acclimatised.

The Azteca held 120,000 all seated, and this was the first time we had seen the 'Mexican wave'. It wasn't a capacity crowd but it was a wonderful and surprising sight that added to the atmosphere. I began to think about how amazing the atmosphere would be when the tournament started for real. I couldn't wait.

We had learned from our training at a very pleasant country club in the hills above Mexico City that the ball travelled further and faster than we were used to because of the thinner air. I practised getting off the ground a shade earlier, effectively waiting for the ball in the air and this was to pay dividends later.

Mark Hateley scored against Italy with a fine goal but the Italians were awarded a dodgy penalty in the final minutes. Even so, we were heartened by the performance. The England team played well enough against Mexico with the players becoming better attuned to the conditions, but we lost by the game's only goal. Mark and the Italy-based players had by now returned to their clubs and I was sent on for the final seven minutes against Mexico. I was given the simple instruction to do what I could which, I'm afraid, wasn't much. But I was pleased to have actually got on to the pitch.

I had not pinned my hopes of playing in the third game against West Germany, even though speculation about my doing so was mounting in the press. I expected to play in the final match against the USA in LA. So when the word came that my first full international appearance would be against West Germany I was walking on air. No one needed to tell me this was going to be a big day for my career, although I tried to keep it all low-key. Inside, I felt nervous, but not as much as I had thought I might do when the moment came. It was probably just as well that I didn't see what was in the papers back home as I might have been trembling in my boots.

Bobby Robson told them, 'He's been chucked in at the deep end and he has to swim. Kerry must not try to do the things he cannot do. He must concentrate on what he is good at. There is a big difference between international and club football and he'll be playing against a system he has never confronted.' We had lost our first three games and it was probably also good for my peace of mind that I didn't know at the time that no England team had ever lost four consecutive games.

The night before my big day, I telephoned my dad, so far away at home in Luton. He advised me to stick strictly to what I did best; it was important to play my normal game, to pass the ball simply and accurately and, if goal-scoring opportunities came my way, to concentrate strongly on keeping my cool.

It is impossible to describe the overwhelming sense of pride I felt when I pulled the England shirt over my head in the dressing room. I'd had seven minutes as a sub in the previous game but this was entirely different. Now I could sit and reflect on the great honour that had been bestowed on me.

As the national anthem sounded around the vast Azteca I was very much aware that, at the age of twenty-three years and eleven months, I was at long last Kerry Dixon of England, and it was no dream, no longer a schoolboy fantasy, wanting to be Bobby Charlton, Tom Finney, Stanley Matthews, Bobby Moore, Geoff Hurst.

The West German team had arrived in Mexico only a couple of days before the game, believing that altitude had little effect in a short time. For a while it looked as though they might have been right as they rained in spectacular shots from all angles, so that Peter Shilton had to be at his considerable best to keep them out. The early pace of the game was hectic and it seemed that Gary Lineker and I were making a lot of runs without actually receiving the ball. The breakthrough arrived when Glenn Hoddle sought me out with a nicely judged chip pass. From a corner of my eye I saw captain Bryan Robson begin one of his characteristic runs into space and instinctively I chested the ball down into his path. About a minute earlier the captain had been guilty of a missed chance to put us ahead when he had scooped his chance over the bar, but this time there was to be no mistake. His finishing was superb, and it was marvellous for me to have contributed to a very fine England goal.

Shortly before half-time the Germans were presented with a golden opportunity to level when Mark Wright pulled down Uwe Rahan, but Shilton dived to his left for a brilliant save.

Some of the other lads required a quick whiff of oxygen

at half-time to relieve their aching lungs but I was feeling in great shape, and more than ready for another forty-five minutes. And just eight minutes into the second half I found myself celebrating the most unforgettable moment of my life. Terry Butcher pushed forward into an attacking position, robbing Klaus Augenthaler, and thundered towards the Germans' penalty area. I raced forward in support and Butcher attempted to go round goalie Harald Schumacher, who touched the ball in my direction. I had an empty goal in front of me but the ball had come at me sharply and, for one horrible moment, got clogged up under my feet before I was able to knock it towards the goal. I wheeled away in sheer excitement and didn't see the shot graze the post. Some people said they thought I had missed, but it went in. I knew it was a goal from the moment I hit the shot.

The Germans were finished, many of them appearing to have reached the point of physical exhaustion. Then in the fifty-seventh minute, even my own wildest dreams were exceeded. John Barnes, my roommate on the tour, had replaced Lineker. He put over a superb cross to the far post and I got the pay-off for the hours I'd spent practising jumping that split-second earlier. I was up there, waiting, when the ball arrived and was able to power a header well beyond the keeper. A second goal... I just couldn't believe it. I kept expecting to wake up at any moment. I could imagine the scenes in the living room of my parents' house back in Luton, the two of them dancing in delight round the television. The rest of the game is now a blur. All I know is that West Germany were well and truly beaten.

Coming off the field at the end I was grabbed by a television interviewer who asked me to describe my feelings. I told him

I was over the moon and got some stick about that from the lads. Of course, I tried to avoid the old clichés but at that moment I couldn't help myself. We had managed the biggest win over West Germany for fifty years. All of us were elated and although Bobby didn't go overboard we could all tell how pleased he was inside.

To me he simply said, 'Well done, son.'

That was all he needed to say. There was no need for him to add anything.

As soon as we returned to the hotel I telephoned my parents, who couldn't disguise their happiness, even though Dad had a headache. Apparently, he'd been even more nervous than me.

We were all in great heart as we moved on to LA. Although the victory over the Germans had encouraged us all and it was said the game with the USA would be much easier I certainly didn't see it that way. I knew we would be crucified in the press if we lost and even if we won by, say, two goals, even that wouldn't go down too well.

I need not have worried as Gary Lineker put us ahead with a quite astonishing goal, a magnificent shot on the volley, and from then on the result was never in doubt. I scored two in a 5–0 win and might have had four if I'd taken all my chances.

'Well done, son, you've had a great tour,' Bobby said as the party left the hotel on Sunset Boulevard to return to England. He was staying behind to visit Colorado in the hope of establishing our training headquarters before the start of the World Cup Finals. I was delighted to read his comments in the papers when I got home. He said, 'We didn't really know Kerry before he came on this trip but he has impressed everyone with his attitude. He's a nice lad and excellent tourist.

He has shown he can get goals at this level and providing he can continue his goal-scoring, from next season he looks the ideal back-up at centre-forward.'

I felt a great satisfaction in having proved the critics wrong, but I knew that there was still a long way for me to go. I had made the breakthrough and now it was all up to me to build on it and return to Mexico as a member of the World Cup squad.

Adding four England goals in two internationals and one in the under-21s, the total for the season came to forty-one. Not bad.

CHAPTER EIGHT

MAN U MAKE A BID

I was committed to Chelsea – I even signed a new four-year contract when I still had a year to go on the old ones. And then came so much upheaval before the season began in 1985 that it seemed nothing was certain any longer.

I thought I was in it for the long term at Chelsea as I trusted the manager, liked the chairman and believed in the vision that the club was going places, but then I heard that John Neal was to be moved to an advisory role and was being replaced as manager by John Hollins, who brought in Ernie Walley as his coach. Walley had, for a brief period, been Crystal Palace manager and was to make an immediate impact with this strict training regime. We soon had a nickname for him – 'Sergeant Major'.

I was deeply disappointed by the change, as John Neal commanded my special respect for having taken such a big chance with me. I owed him, big time. The new manager telephoned me at home and congratulated me warmly for the success I had achieved with England during the summer tour, and then business with Chelsea continued as usual.

After some gruelling pre-season under Ernie the new coach told me that his regime would make me so much fitter I'd be a permanent fixture in the England team. He said I needed plenty of practice in holding up the ball, shielding it from defenders and in quick-turning. It seemed to me that he was beginning to pick on me, and as it continued it began to become irritating and I became suspicious.

At length I requested a meeting and demanded to know if he rated me as a player. He was a bit taken aback but said that of course he did. I put it to him that he was always on my back, and he didn't mince his words in reply. 'Because you're a lazy so-and-so, that's why. You have got everything going for you but you have got to work hard to attain the highest levels.'

Well, I have always respected people who tell me things to my face, and I began to knuckle down. Later in the season, the fruits of hard work with Ernie would become evident when England and Arsenal coach Don Howe and Bobby Robson went on to compliment me on the way I was turning defenders. They asked if I had been practising the move; that made all the hard work worthwhile.

But that was all to come. To begin with, I failed to score in Chelsea's opening five games of the season. Suddenly, what I had achieved in my first season the previous season counted for nothing. We still won three and drew two of those games, and I broke my barren spell at Tottenham with a chip over Ray Clemence when he rushed off his line.

We played Luton in September on the synthetic surface

at Kenilworth Road with Mick Harford making a name for himself for our opponents at centre-forward. He opened the scoring with a spectacular volley but I got the equaliser. In the next match I scored against Peter Shilton and I was also up against England centre-half Mark Wright. I scored in our first away win of the season at Manchester City, where their manager praised my partnership with David Speedie. He thought we made a tremendous pair who understood each other well; in his opinion he said, we made the best duo in football.

I scored a couple in the second leg of the Milk Cup against Mansfield, making four goals in my last three games. I felt I back on track and all the talk was of comparisons with Gary Lineker. By this time Gary and Frank McAvvenie were joint top scorers each with four more than me. I headed the opening goal as we beat the reigning League champions at the Bridge. Neville Southall was booked for protesting at a penalty award for tripping Speedo, and n was later sent off for a second bookable offence when he handled outside the area to stop me. Speedo scored the second and we won 2–1.

Our next game was against Oxford United who had been promoted to the First Division and were managed by Maurice Evans, the man who had brought me into professional football. I scored, but Oxford eventually won the game with what I have to admit was a great strike by former Chelsea player Peter Rhoades-Brown. Still, we remained at third in the table.

Next up was a match against Manchester United, which came in the middle of intense speculation about my future. Man U were managed by Ron Atkinson who, it was said, wanted to buy me. I was still not entirely confident that John

Hollins really rated me and eventually I had to go to him to check. He said there was nothing to the rumours. Ken Bates himself later said that there had been an approach but he'd told them he wanted £5 million for me!

We played Man U at the Bridge in front of a huge crowd. We were 1–1 when I thought I had scored after I hit a sweet shot that rattled the underside of the bar, but it was not to be and they won 2–1. For the second home game we played against ten men when Graeme Hogg was sent off for two bookable offences, yet a brilliant strike from Mark Hughes won them the match as United continued their march to the top, while we dropped to fifth.

I scored the winning goal as we edged past Fulham in the Milk Cup, and we went on to win four games on the bounce in the League. The first came at Ipswich when I hit one of the best I'd ever scored – their keeper Paul Cooper remarked afterwards it was the greatest goal against him and Ipswich's Terry Butcher, who was watching the game, was equally impressed.

However, despite being in top form, I had not been selected for England, even as a sub against Romania in September or against Turkey in October in an emphatic win that kept England on course to qualify for the World Cup Finals. There was no explanation as to why I wasn't included at the time, but at least I remained in the England squad, and I kept playing to the best of my ability. After the win over the Turks, Bobby Robson took me to one side and said he intended to play me in the final qualifier against Northern Ireland, coming up in November. He had believed I needed the experience of playing at Wembley and had kept me off the subs' bench in previous matches because he wanted me to play from the start of this match.

I knew he would be watching when Chelsea played Nottingham Forest just a few days before the England match. I was determined not to let him down. Nigel Clough and our new signing, Mickey Hazard, each scored, but I hit two, bringing my tally for the season to thirteen in a win that stopped Forest claiming an eighth successive victory.

Playing for England at Wembley should have been another dream fulfilled – but it turned out to be more of a nightmare. The journalists seemed to have it in for me from the start even though I was on my guard. The Northern Irish had to avoid defeat to ensure that they too would qualify for the World Cup Finals, and as England were already sure of a place, the press were keen to find any signs of a fix. As Big Pat Jennings was particularly hopeful about playing in the Finals at the age of forty-one, one journo said to me that it would break Jennings's heart if Northern Ireland didn't make it, and I said that I supposed it would.

The papers duly printed, '"I'll break Jennings' heart," vows Dixon.' I cringed with such embarrassment that I was reluctant to join the other players for breakfast. It was a shame as I had trusted one or two of the journalists. Some time later I met up with Pat at a charity function and apologised for what had appeared. He told me not to worry – he'd been in the game long enough to know that we are all susceptible to the manipulations of journalists anxious for a sensationalised story.

As for the game itself, the press had it in for me again when I missed a couple of chances. A beautiful pass from Glenn

Hoddle gave me the opportunity to get in a header but, instead of glancing the ball, I went for power to beat Pat and it went woefully wide. When I later thought I had scored with a fierce header, Pat made one of his seemingly impossible saves.

So much for me breaking Pat Jennings's heart – he broke mine.

But I was pleased for Pat and Northern Ireland when they got a draw to qualify for the Finals, and I was looking forward to making amends in the team with a friendly against Egypt in Cairo early in the new year. My next Chelsea game was at Newcastle on 16 November and I was treated to the usual kind of stick the Geordie fans dished out, particularly as Chelsea hadn't won at St James' Park for fourteen years.

Glenn Roeder opened the scoring for Newcastle, with Speedo equalising and as we hadn't done enough by half-time we received a deserved roasting from our manager. But we came back in the second half. One of my attempts was fumbled by the keeper, Nigel Spackman followed up to score and I scored late on to celebrate my hundredth League game for Chelsea in style, my sixty-second goal for the club and Chelsea's breaking of the St James' Park jinx.

With that win we regained third place. We had high hopes in our Milk Cup campaign, although our home match with Everton ended in a draw. The contest for the first ever Full Members Cup was in full swing and, after victories over Portsmouth, Charlton and West Brom we had Oxford over two legs to win the southern area final and qualify to play the northern winners. John Aldridge was on the mark, but so was I with my first hat-trick of the season and the eighth of my career so far. Ken Bates promised that if we were in the final he would underwrite the guarantees necessary to persuade the Wembley Stadium authorities to stage the national final, which was typical of the man. My old friend Maurice Evans was very complimentary. He noted the criticism I'd had but was encouraging about the way I just ploughed on scoring goals. I was delighted for him when Oxford went on to win the Milk Cup at Wembley that season.

I travelled to Paris with Howard Kendall to collect my Golden Boot for being the joint top scorer with Gary Lineker the previous season. Howard was collecting the Team of the Year award for Everton and representing Gary. It was a few days before our cup replay with Everton and when we parted company, Howard joked, 'Take it easy in the reply. We can do without those early goals of yours.' As it turned out, I hit an early shot off the far post and scored! Sorry, Howard... Gary scored his sixteenth of the season to equalise, but our Joe McLaughlin drove in the winner.

There was a huge crowd at the Bridge for the last game of the year, against Tottenham on 28 December. I put a header past Ray Clemence, then hit a post and Nigel scored from the penalty spot to put us into second place, two points behind mighty Manchester United.

We were looking good in the cups and the League as we faced Liverpool in the FA Cup on 26 January live on TV. I was feeling confident, and thought that I might get the better of Alan Hansen and Mark Lawrenson. But after just six minutes, as I contested a high ball, took off from the left foot and twisted in mid-air, I felt an excruciating pain in my stomach. I slumped down on the pitch. I couldn't move my legs at all. This was serious. I raised my arm to signal my distress to the bench and was carried by stretcher into the dressing room.

The club doctor decided I was in too much pain to attempt an immediate examination and advised me to take a bath first. But I still couldn't move, not at all. I certainly wasn't able to drag myself over to the team bath. I couldn't even raise my head and shoulders. I tried and tried, but there was simply no response. And in my stomach, that agonising ache.

Mum, Dad and Brian Roach had also realised something was badly wrong and joined us in the dressing room. Nobody could do anything for me. I couldn't even say at that point what the problem was. The ambulance arrived shortly after half-time. As I was leaving the Bridge I heard that David Speedie had scored a magnificent goal but Liverpool were leading 2–1. All the way to the hospital I prayed that somehow Chelsea would snatch an equaliser, as I was sure I would be fit for the reply.

The doctors carried out tests, looking for a hernia or perhaps a rupture. At last they detected a torn stomach muscle that had affected the groin area and, from there, the whole of my left side. To add to the bad news, I heard that we had been beaten by Liverpool. I was to stay in hospital for further observation. The doctors said that it was likely that I would not play for at least a month – and would be on the sidelines much longer. As the truth of the situation filtered through I felt devastated. I still hoped, however, that it wouldn't affect my England selection.

I limped along to the vital Milk Cup replay against QPR the following Wednesday, to watch us go out of the cup with a 2–0 defeat. The only positive note was that due to postponements because of the wintry weather, I wasn't missing too many games. The key question was when I would risk a comeback.

In early February, a fortnight before the next England international in Israel, Bobby Robson inevitably asked me if I would be fit enough for the squad. The doctor had told me that, in theory, I should have recovered sufficiently, but my actual level of match fitness was debatable. Robson asked John Hollins if he would play me for the club. Hollins said he would and that was good enough for the England manager. I wasn't sure myself and thought about withdrawing, although I wanted to travel with the squad even if I couldn't actually play. The advice I was getting elsewhere was mixed, with people coming down on both sides.

On the Sunday night before the Israel game I made up my mind. I reported to the England team hotel in Luton and went immediately to Robson's room. I told him that I was not match-fit, and he said that, nevertheless, he wanted me to play. He knew my medical situation but still believed it was important for me to take part. He stressed that it would not influence him in the future if I was unable to complete a full match.

I went back to my room to mull over what had been said. I knew that Mick Harford of Luton Town was in top form and manager David Pleat and the press were campaigning for his inclusion – just as they once had for me. I couldn't afford to take the risk of dropping out of the squad and allow him to take my place. Yet the injury had been a bad one, wrenching the muscles around the pelvis from the bone; even when you are young, such injuries don't heal quickly.

From the moment we started training sessions in Israel I was conscious of the restriction in my mobility. When we started playing the game itself I struggled through the first half, feeling a shadow of myself with Peter Beardsley playing alongside me in place of an injured Gary Lineker. Israel caught us out with a shock early goal, but Bryan Robson levelled with a stupendous right-foot volley from a marvellous Glenn Hoddle pass. Shortly afterwards I was taken off. Robson scored the winner from the penalty spot.

I wasn't sure I had made the right decision to play but Robson eased my mind during the five-hour flight back, and told me that I would be named in the squad for the next game in Russia.

My first game back for Chelsea was at home to Manchester City in early March. I felt less than convinced I was back to normal, at least mentally – I was scared the muscle would go again, and I was probably slower than usual. But the manager was superb, resisting the temptation to play me in the reserves. He took a gamble by continuing to play me in the First Division games at a time when he could ill afford to take risks – we still had a chance for the title. Yet my form remained poor.

The final of the Full Members Cup was to be played at Wembley on Sunday 23 March, with a friendly against the USSR the following Wednesday. Naturally, my club wanted me to play and I could hardly complain after Ken Bates had gone to so much trouble to guarantee that the Full Members games would be staged at Wembley. Hateley and Lineker were anyway the first-choice England strikers, and the England manager had no choice other than to comply with club wishes.

I picked up a slight groin strain in the Saturday League

game with Southampton. The press were quick to suggest that this latest injury was connected to the serious muscle damage and that this was why I was struggling to make a comeback, but I felt that they were well off the mark. Even so, I had a fitness test on the Wembley pitch an hour before kick-off and the manager and I decided together that it would be best not to risk incurring further damage. Speedo hit a hat-trick and Colin Lee replaced me to grab a couple of goals and, despite a remarkable comeback by Manchester City, we won 5–4.

Hateley, by now with AC Milan, also went down with an injury and that meant I would have been able to play in the friendly – Sod's Law. Instead, Lineker and Beardsley began to play as a team without the input of the usual No. 9. Their explosive running provided a different dimension to the game. Beardsley set up a winning goal with a marvellous tackle on the edge of the Russian penalty area before placing the ball in the path of Chris Waddle to score, the first defeat suffered on home soil by the Russians for seven years. Robson began to see that if he wanted to change the formation he could go for Beardsley as an alternative to Hateley, rather than me.

The following Sunday was the day of Chelsea's London derby with West Ham, who fancied their title chances as much as we did. There was acres of coverage in the run-up to the game, much of it centring on whether the manager might keep faith with Colin Lee while I was not fully fit. They also alleged that I was unhappy because I suspected that John Hollins didn't really rate me, and that I might be considering my position at the club. Not surprisingly, I began to wonder myself what was going on.

I spoke with John Hollins and declared myself fit to play, but when he named the team I was not included. I went to see him again. He explained that I was unfit to train for most of the week and he couldn't see any point in rushing me back into the team for one game. I would be risking a breakdown when he would need me for many more games before the end of the season. I understood the logic of the decision, particularly when he assured me that I would be in the team, no matter what, against QPR on the following Monday.

Colin Lee again took my place at the Bridge against the Hammers, who were outstanding as they beat Chelsea 4–0. That night I was inundated with calls from reporters asking me to comment on the suggestion that the manager had said I had been fit to play in the match but simply hadn't been selected. I chose to say nothing, but the following morning the papers were full of the story. Naturally, I felt confused and angry.

That morning I went to the training ground where I found Ernie Waley and I told him that I believed Chelsea wanted me out. Ernie went into the manager's office to telephone John Hollins, who insisted that he had not been quoted accurately. He explained that he had allowed the press to interpret the situation as they saw fit, adding that I should understand the kind of tricks newspaper reporters were capable of getting up to because I had suffered myself in the past. He assured me once again that I would be in the team on Monday. I accepted what he had to say as I wasn't looking for a row. Even so, I remained disturbed by the entire business.

Easter Monday, 31 March, came at Loftus Road, where the manager kept his word – I was in the team. We were beaten

6–0; not a day to remember. Perhaps I'd have been better off not being included!

After a draw at Ipswich we were off to face Manchester United at Old Trafford, where Big Ron was suffering a poor run and their hopes of the title were receding. They needed to beat us to stand any chance of getting back on track. We were pummelled throughout the first half, attack after attack from a United side determined to make an impact in front of a huge crowd. In the second half, I took a pass in the centre circle and was off down the middle, the adrenalin flowing. I felt confident, using my pace to hold off the defenders. The killer instinct returned as I looked up, measured the distance that goalkeeper Chris Turner had come off his line and slipped the ball beyond him for one of the finest goals I had scored.

Then, from a Speedo cross, I swept the ball into the net, the old predatory instinct fully effective once more. I'd never scored against United before, and the rumours about them making a move for me only added to my feelings of success. I was elated. I had emerged from a long, dark and lonely tunnel, and I remain convinced that those two goals at Old Trafford put me on the road to Mexico.

I was sure Bobby Robson would come to watch when we played West Ham at Upton Park in mid-April, but in the event it turned out to be Don Howe. I didn't score but I managed an assist with a cross for Pat Nevin to clinch the winner, to take us to third place in the League. By the time Liverpool arrived at the Bridge on 3 May we were well adrift and they needed to win to land the title for Kenny Dalglish in his first season as a player-manager. He was a superb player and goal-scorer, claiming the winner with a classic Dalglish finish; he ran into our area, controlled the ball on his chest and then volleyed into the far corner. Liverpool collected the League championship and FA Cup Double with a brilliant victory over Everton in the first-ever all-Merseyside final at Wembley. Chelsea finished the season in sixth place.

Competition for the final World Cup selection was now fierce and I was extremely nervous about my own position in the England side. I found myself scribbling down lists of players and attempting to settle on a final selection. It was going to be important to get into the squad for a game against Scotland at Wembley as the manager was to name his World Cup squad on the following Monday. The manager did keep his word although, as I had suspected I would be, I was on the bench. Lineker had been injured playing for Everton and there was some talk I'd be picked to play alongside Hateley, but in the end Trevor Francis was called up for his first international for almost a year.

All the players were measured for their World Cup suits the day before the game, and I remember thinking to myself that if I was eventually to be left out I would be unable to recover from the sheer embarrassment. Francis went on to play well enough, but failed to score as we beat the Scots 2–1 with goals from Terry Butcher and Glenn Hoddle. This was England's ninth game without defeat.

Bobby Robson was planning to name twenty-two players to travel to Colorado for World Cup preparation, and when the names appeared early in a couple of newspapers I refused to believe what I read until the day the selection was officially announced. I was a bundle of nerves by the time the day of reckoning arrived. But there it was.

Kerry Dixon was going to Mexico.

It was a huge relief. I felt sorry for outstanding players such as Tony Woodcock and Trevor Francis who failed to make the cut. Francis complained bitterly in the press about the way he had been treated and I knew how devastated I would have been if I hadn't been included. I also knew that I would not completely believe it until I actually set foot on the aircraft. But if, somehow, it really did happen, this would be the proudest chapter of my life no matter what happened in Mexico.

It was the night before the last club game, against Watford, after which I was heading straight off to join England, when Brian Roach phoned to warn me about a *Daily Mirror* story to be headlined DIXON AXED. According to the journalist, I was being replaced at Chelsea by new striker Gordon Durie, who had be signed from Hibernians for £400,000. I already knew the club was anxious to try him out before the end of the season and paid little attention. I was more excited about the World Cup in Mexico.

The story appeared as described the following morning and during the pre-match meal I was pulled to one side by the manager with kick-off just ninety minutes way. John Hollins said that as I was going to the World Cup he did indeed intend to leave me out so he could try a couple of new tactics. I insisted I wanted to play in the game. But he was equally determined to see the new boy in the team system with wingers Paul Canoville and Kevin McAllister.

I felt angry, disappointed and dismayed, all at the same time. Harsh words were exchanged, but it was a done deal. But why, I wanted to know, did the press know about team selection before I did? He told me they had merely been guessing. Good guess! I retorted, and left the room.

I had a lot of hard thinking to do over the summer while I was away with England. I already knew that as soon as the World Cup was over, I would be seeking another meeting with the Chelsea manager.

CHAPTER NINE

WORLD CUP MEXICO

I was filled with hope, ambition, and expectancy when I joined up with the England squad at Heathrow airport on 6 May 1986. It was a good day all round, actually, as I had just signed a new sponsorship deal with a car rental company including an agreement that I would be supplied with a Ford Granada Ghia. That kind of deal was special, a real treat, and it got me interested in the concept of car rental – I wondered if that could be a business opportunity for me some time. Everything seemed exciting and possible. I was at the top of the football tree and loving every minute of it. Life was exciting, how could it fail to be? I was off to the World Cup.

The night before the flight we attended a government reception before going back to the hotel at 8 p.m. for a very good dinner. I went up to the room I was sharing with my good friend John Barnes for an early bedtime, but sleep didn't come easily that night. Hardly surprising, with all the excitement and expectation ahead. I lay awake, the adrenalin flowing, and my thoughts turned to years earlier, as if a movie of my whole life was running through my mind. All the practice with Dad; the clips around the ear from Mum when she believed I wasn't taking my responsibilities seriously enough; the pain and humiliation of rejection by my home team Luton; being turned away by Tottenham when even my ability to score didn't seem enough, to the happy days with Dunstable, the fight back at Reading and the goals that made me a success at Chelsea; and, finally, making it as an England international.

I thought of my parents again. Mike and Anne Dixon: their son was on his way to the World Cup with England. The thought of them being so excited for me made me very happy, knowing how proud they were of me. If it hadn't been for them I would have been stuck in an engineering factory in Luton, rushing home from work to catch the World Cup games on TV. My overriding feeling was one of gratitude for what they had done. Whenever I was asked by interviewers or aspiring young players how to reach the top in football I would say, 'A bit of talent and a mum and dad like mine and you won't go far wrong.' I had been very fortunate to enjoy and prosper from the support, love and devotion of a closely knit family.

My mum, dad, sister, grandparents, aunties, uncles and mates I had known since schooldays had been behind me every step up to this point. I felt I was repaying that faith in me in a small way by my success on the football pitch, playing for my country and going to the World Cup Finals. I knew Mark Hateley was first choice for the No. 9 shirt but, although I felt I would peak at the 1990 Finals, I still wanted to get into the team.

I made an embarrassing start to my bid for inclusion when my holdall provided by Umbro (who provided all the kit and suits for the team and the media), developed a split in its side. The press photographers were out in force, as you might expect, and the TV camera crews followed our every move; with all the goings-on, the intensity of the media coverage, you knew this was it, the sheer importance of the greatest football show on earth.

After an eight-hour flight to the USA, a wait of two hours at St Louis airport and another two-hour flight to Colorado Springs, we began our two-week acclimatisation programme for the heat and altitude we would experience in Mexico. Scorching sun? Blistering heat? Dehydration? We woke up to snow!

The Broadmoor Hotel, a haven to us for the next couple of weeks, was an unbelievable place, with breath-taking views of the Rocky Mountains. There was a lake, two championship golf courses, an outdoor skating rink, four gourmet restaurants and a lovely swimming pool. It was a shame to leave the place for our training at the US Air Force Academy up in the hills, though the set-up there was pretty spectacular in itself, and included a swimming pool and sauna facilities to help build up the resistance of the body to high temperatures. We walked three miles up the mountain to test out the altitude when the weather improved. Mark Hateley, Glenn Hoddle, Kenny Sansom and myself ran down the mountain, dodging the rocks, then into the steam room to build up temperature resistance.

On Saturday, 10 May I woke early by local time, but mid-afternoon back home, and telephoned home to hear the news before the FA Cup Final. I was shocked to hear that Speedo had been left out of the Scotland World Cup squad as I understood that he had been promised a place by manager Alex Ferguson. I felt terribly sorry for him. It was tough enough sweating to get your place, but having been promised one only not to be selected was hard even for someone as tough as Speedo.

The England players held a sweep on the first goal-scorer in the final between Everton and Liverpool. I drew Ian Rush, and was well pleased with that, of course. Then news filtered through that Lineker scored for Everton and I felt ready to throttle Gary when he arrived in the USA! Liverpool went on to win 3–1 and Rush scored twice – just my luck. This was, perhaps, an early indication of my fortune regarding gambling. I wish I had heeded the warning signs back then, but we were all at it in the England camp. Whether a little flutter or something more involved, the guys sitting next to each other during dinner were invariably into something and winning – or, more likely, losing. We later got to watch a video of the final and it whetted my appetite to play in one myself. In the event, I never did.

I might not have been winning any pounds on the Cup Final sweep, but I had, surprisingly, put on four pounds in weight. So it was now time to resist all the snacks and the chips, at a time when there wasn't the focus on diet that players have today. Now nutrition plays a pivotal part in preparation but while we were out there, some of the others put on six pounds, despite the heat and the ninety minute daily training sessions. For a while we had to virtually stop eating.

Kerry celebrates scoring in the Arsenal v Chelsea match at Highbury, 25 August 1984.

(© S&G/S&G and Barratts/EMPICS Sport)

Left: My father and mother holding me and my sister Jane. My family have been my greatest help and support throughout my life and career.

Centre: Jane and me on a day out with the family – I was already football mad, and would later be in great demand as the owner of a proper ball.

Below: Being paid, both as an apprentice toolmaker and as a part-time player, brought benefits – Jane and me standing beside my first car, a Ford Capri.

Above: Signing for Chelsea in August 1983, watched by Sheila Marson, the club ecretary, and Ian McNeill, the assistant manager.

Below: The Player of the Year 1983–4 Season Awards held in May 1984 at the Café Royal in London. From left to right: David Speedie, Pat Nevin, Chelsea chairman Ken Bates and Kerry Dixon.

(© Hugh Hastings/Chelsea FC via Getty Images)

Above: 'Everything was going great until I slipped in some mud during a game just before Christmas and overstretched… I feared for my career as this was my first serious injury.'

(© Chelsea FC/Getty Images)

Below: 'Golden Boy' – waiting to go on for Chelsea during his first season with the club in 1983.

(© Chelsea FC via Getty Images/Getty Images)

Above: Holding my son, Joe, in company with my friend Christian Seunig from Austria. Much later in life, Joe has been a tower of strength, like all my family.

Below: Kerry celebrates scoring the winning goal in a 1–0 win over QPR at Stamford Bridge, in a First Division match on 6 April 1985.

Left: Kerry playing in another First Division match, Chelsea v Manchester United, 26 October 1985.

(© PA/PA Archive/Press Association Images)

Below: Kerry playing for England against the host team on 9 June 1985, during the pre-World Cup tour of Mexico.

(© Peter Robinson/EMPICS Sport)

Top left: Kerry playing against Middlesbrough in the Full Members Cup final, 25 March 1990; Chelsea won 1–0.

(© Neal Simpson/EMPICS Sport)

Top right: Kerry and David Speedie during their days at Southampton, 1 January 1992. The two had been a formidable pairing at Chelsea, but had less success at the south coast club.

(© Ben Radford/Allsport)

Below left: Kerry at the Southern Masters in Milton Keynes, 22 June 2003.

(© Andy Couldridge/Action Images)

Below right: 'As I was walking out of those doors I made the decision that I would never be returning.' Kerry was met by Kim and his son Joe; the feeling of freedom was amazing.

(© Kim White)

Above: Chelsea's all-time highest goal scorers: (from left to right) Frank Lampard (211), Bobby Tambling (202) and Kerry Dixon (193). *(© Chelsea FC via Getty Images/Getty Images)*

Below: Kerry relaxing during conversations with his co-author in 2016, part of his drawing a line under his past life to start a fresh one. *(© Poppy Harris)*

We played a warm-up against the US Air Force. Mark scored a hat-trick in the first half, I started the second half and matched him for what turned out to be an 11–0 win. As the build-up continued I played and scored a couple in the second half of a 4–1 win against South Korea. Coach Don Howe and the manager commented on my improvement in turning defenders, which made me feel really good about myself and gave me renewed hope I would be playing some part in England's World Cup games.

We took a six-hour flight to LA for the next game, against Mexico. Mark started, and I was disappointed in that. He collected two great goals, enough to book his place for the World Cup opener against Portugal. Peter Beardsley scored another, but I only got on the pitch for the last seventeen minutes.

Wives and girlfriends arrived at once we were back at the Broadmoor, among them my girlfriend Michele. She soon began to suffer stomach pains and Gary Stevens's girlfriend fainted after breakfast; both were danger signs of the effects of heat and altitude. Our partners departed on the day we headed off to Vancouver for an 11 a.m. kick-off against Canada in front of a crowd of 7,000. Shockingly, Gary Lineker was rushed to hospital with a suspected broken wrist. We wondered if he might miss the Finals, but the diagnosis was a sprain. Peter Beardsley replaced him – to a great reception, as he once played for the Vancouver Whitecaps. Mark scored again in the 1–0 win to cement his place as England's first-choice No. 9.

We returned to Broadmoor to prepare for Mexico – a flight to LA followed by a five-hour wait for a flight to Monterrey.

We were still on the runway when another passenger began ranting and raving that his luggage had not been loaded. Looking out of the window, we could all see not just one but all our bags still on the tarmac. We were told, not reassuringly, that because of the weight most of the luggage was to be sent on later. Mid-flight we were hit by turbulence and an electrical storm, with the plane suffering some huge dips in altitude that felt like being on a roller-coaster. A half-hour from our destination the captain calmly informed us that fuel was running low and he was going to have to land or ditch some of the luggage. I'm sure I heard someone suggest we should ditch the reporters at the back of the plane – but, no, surely not! Goalkeeper Chris Woods was never a good flyer at the best of times and now he was as a white as a sheet. We ploughed on, and the plane began losing height rapidly to make its approach for landing, with Glenn Hoddle shouting that he couldn't see the runaway – and if someone with his brilliant vision couldn't see it we were in deep trouble. Some of the lads began to panic big time. We landed safely at LA, yet we were all very aware that we had only a break before we had another flight.

It was pandemonium when we finally got to Monterrey, with TV crews everywhere– you couldn't move for them. At least the final part of the journey was by coach – sixty miles up into the hills to our headquarters in Saltillo. This was apparently bandit country. Six police cars escorted our coach. Every time we left for training in Monterrey and returned, there was a convoy. Armed guards travelled in one bus, journalists were in another and we were accompanied by our own armed guards, their guns poking out the windows in case the bandits came down from the hills after our money and our blood. The old vehicles went as fast as they could and police had every road and every side track cordoned off.

Our hotel, the Camino Real, was simply magnificent, a wonderful haven in the middle of nowhere, offering perfect tranquillity in which to focus on preparation. You hear so much these days about players being bored on World Cup or Euro duty. It's tragic to hear it – sad and it makes me think that they are now too full of a sense of entitlement. We were overjoyed to be in Mexico and wanted to focus on nothing but the games. Boredom never came into it. I cannot imagine that sort of attitude. For me, to be there was a privilege, and I was totally dedicated to trying to force my way into Bobby Robson's thinking to ensure a place in the team or, failing that, a place among the substitutes.

The heat and humidity in training were something else, and we all would have had plenty to complain about if we had wanted to, but there was just the usual banter and fun. In my first session I lost six pounds. I've never been so light. I felt sick, giddy and woozy on the coach journey back. Our doctor, Vernon Edwards, diagnosed heat exhaustion and I had to drink plenty of our stock of purified water and two cans of orange juice before I felt better.

You certainly get to know your teammates when you spend so much time together. Beardsley was the organiser, Steve Hodge the most forgetful, not knowing what to wear on special occasions. He also lost a sweater and even the key to his locker. They called me Ernie, thanks to my Ernie Wise hairstyle, so they said. I was not impressed by that comparison.

Bobby Robson always muddled up our names– he was

infamous for that, and rightly so. It came to a head when he called Bryan Robson 'Bobby' and Bryan had to tell him, 'No, I'm Bryan – you're Bobby.' It was also on this tour that the manager began to call Peter Shilton 'Shilly' in every training session, and the nickname stuck.

We practised against a local team, who had just won the Mexican club championship, but the game took on extra significance when we heard it was to be televised back home. The manager said he wanted to give some of the squad players a crack, so I rang Mum and Dad and told them to watch out for me: 'I've got a big chance now.' They wished me all the best. Dad gave me the usual advice – keep it simple and if the chance of a goal comes along to go for it, a strategy that had worked well for me over the last few years. I knew they would be rooting for me and I didn't want to let them down. I scored the first two goals and made one for my roommate Barnsey. Gary Stevens got the last goal in a 4–1 win. After the interviews and autograph signing, I weighed in and found that I was five pounds lighter.

Bobby Robson called the players together to let us know that Dr Edwards, who had become a great pal, had been taken ill during the match; he had suffered a heart attack and was rushed into intensive care in Monterrey hospital. The happy mood among the players evaporated; there was hardly a sound on the team bus back to Saltillo. During dinner that evening the manager told us that the doc had suffered a massive heart attack and his wife was being informed. We weren't given many details but the atmosphere at the meal was muted, with none of the jokes and fooling around that usually characterised these gatherings. Next morning there was some better news – our team doctor's condition had improved and we were cheered up.

The weather was terrible, with constant rain, and the following day the Monterrey pitch was water-logged and training cancelled. I was glad, really, as I didn't feel too well. We trained on the pitch in Saltillo instead but this too was heavy and sticky, with much water. I developed a headache and sore throat. I saw the stand-in doctor, who prescribed tablets and told me to inhale over steaming water to clear my sinuses. I was ordered to stay in my room while the squad went off to an official function in Monterrey.

World Cup holders Italy played Bulgaria in the first match of the Finals. Everyone wanted to watch it, but I was stuck inhaling steam in my room. Italy should have won but Bulgaria equalised in the last five minutes.

We continued to train, now at Portugal's headquarters in Saltillo as our opening game opponents were across the road from our hotel. We played a team of twelve-year-olds as a public relations exercise.

Bobby Robson named the team for the opening game, and it was no great surprise. It was the team we all expected, and I was not in it. But a couple of days later, the manager named his substitutes, and again I was not among them. Now I was really disappointed – depressed, in fact.

The opening game in Monterrey was a disaster for England, losing to a Portugal side that had fielded a five-man midfield aiming for a draw and got away with an unexpected win. The Portugal camp had been in total disarray in the weeks leading up to the game, with players refusing to train and even threatening a strike over unpaid bonuses and broken promises.

Yet they looked fit enough and motivated enough when they beat England. 'Not over yet, lift up your heads,' said Bobby Robson in a very gloomy dressing room afterwards.

Still, the following day it was Derby Day at Epsom, and Kenny Samson and Glenn Hoddle were the bookies – they had already been taking our bets on the World Cup games. I backed Dancing Brave and it finished second – pretty much the story of my life.

I could certainly have had another bet on who would be in the next team. It was the same again. Bobby Robson showed his faith in using the same squad to take on Morocco, and it would have been a win under normal circumstances. But this was not normal – the heat had now been turned up and the pressure was full on after losing the opening game. We were shielded from the reaction as we were so far from home, yet we all sensed that there would be a deluge of negative press back in England. Whenever one of us rang home we got a slight flavour of the adverse commentary.

I had a glass of orange juice with Dave Faulder, a fan from Luton. I thought I might as well relax and not worry – the manager said he didn't plan to announce the subs until the day of the game. The weather gave me an opportunity to get a nice tan to go home with, even if it was a handicap for those playing. But this also proved tricky, as sunbathing was banned after 11.15 a.m. and, on the day of the game, banned altogether.

Once again, when the time came I was left out of the subs on what was another day of disaster for the England team. Ray Wilkins was sent off for throwing the ball in the direction of the Paraguayan ref, although a goalless draw was reasonable under the circumstances of playing with ten men for so long in that heat.

England now had to beat Poland in the final game to stay in the World Cup. When we had first seen our group we thought it would be reasonably straightforward to navigate – no one had imagined it would turn out like this. The travelling England supporters were bitterly disappointed and some turned a bit nasty as we boarded the coach on our way back from the game, shaking their fists at us and throwing the Union Jack flags to the ground in disgust. Bobby Robson called a team meeting after dinner. He laid it on the line; we had to beat Poland and he was sure that we would.

The manager opted to announce his team on the day of the game and called a meeting at 11.30 a.m. I was not selected, as Lineker-Beardsley remained Robson's favoured partnership, but at least this time I was one of the subs. Peter Reid replaced suspended Ray Wilkins, Steve Hodge was in for Bryan Robson and Trevor Steven called up in a tactical change.

Gary Lineker went on to hit a fabulous hat-trick against Poland. A five-man move, started by Glenn Hoddle, brought his first goal in just eight minutes. The second goal was even better, with Kenny Sansom, Beardsley and Hodge creating the chance, and Lineker's third came after just thirty-five minutes. Six minutes from time I made my World Cup debut coming on for Lineker, my seventh cap for England. I had a friendly rivalry with Gary and he was always a good bloke, wishing me well as I took my place. I got into a good position in which I was sure I would score, but the ball failed to arrive.

The England fans danced a victory conga on the terraces, a far cry from their anger when we looked to be out of the

Finals. We qualified in second place in Group F and had to move to Mexico City to face Paraguay in the last sixteen. It was an ecstatic atmosphere on the coach back to Saltillo, where we were applauded into our hotel by the staff. The party thrown that evening by Umbro set the celebratory mood.

We were sorry to be leaving the hugely friendly and welcoming Camino Real and were not impressed with Mexico City nor our hotel, the Valle de Mexico. All the TV channels were Mexican. At least we had our own videos and books, and I found an indoor tennis court next door to the hotel where I played for two hours with Barnsey, Chris Waddle and Chris Woods.

Somehow, in chasing the ball trying to make a return, I managed to hit myself in the face with my own racquet. There was blood everywhere and I needed stitches for the wound between my eyes. I was horrified at the thought that such a stupid thing would put me out of contention for the Paraguay match, and even more fearful of what the manager might think of it all. The doctor, John Crane, put four stitches in the wound, assisted by physios Fred Street and Norman Medhurst.

As you would expect, a group of the lads gathered outside the medical room and had a good old laugh at my expense. I just hoped the manager would find it funny, although I doubted it. I felt a right idiot and had to put up with all the jibes. The date was Friday 13 June... Fortunately, it was clear next morning at breakfast, that Bobby Robson did find it all very amusing, and he too made fun of me. That was a huge relief. At training – a lovely spot just outside of the city at the ground owned by a team called Reforma – the doc had to wash my hair while I held a waterproof gauze over my gash. Cue more mickey-taking.

We moved hotel as there was too much noise and ended up at the Holiday Inn. We also finally got to train at the Azteca, where Barnsey and Ray Wilkins washed my hair for me. Embarrassing, or what? The Italian team shared the same hotel and were busy moaning about being away from home too long; not the best of attitudes when they were due to face France the next day. Maybe it was a sign of the times, for players were starting to be constantly dissatisfied, even about playing at the very highest level in the World Cup. Perhaps it was only me who had a different approach. I was just delighted to be there.

Meanwhile, I was on my usual losing run with bookies Hoddle and Sansom. I seemed to be the kiss of death for any team I backed and yet I went on betting – a real sign of things to come in my gambling. I wagered that Argentina and Uruguay would draw, and Argentina won 1–0. And, of course, we would have to play Argentina if we beat Paraguay.

Robson picked virtually the same team against Paraguay, the exception being Alvin Martin replacing the suspended Terry Fenwick (he had collected three yellow cards, two of them in the Portugal game). The choice was no surprise as the manager could hardly have changed a team that performed against the Poles with such sparkle, and in doing so dug England out of an enormous hole against the Poles.

The planning was for penalty shoot-outs, although he didn't yet name the subs, but I took a few penalties in the practice sessions just in case. It was said that you couldn't replicate the atmosphere and pressure of the match itself but I wanted to take it seriously, particularly when the stakes could be so high. I was never that great, actually – Graham Roberts was the best penalty-taker I ever saw. He would later score about thirteen in the year Chelsea were promoted. I don't think he missed any. I was hit-or-miss by contrast. Blast them, place them, I did whatever came into my mind at the time.

Back at the hotel I backed Italy to beat France, and of course Michel Platini scored a cracker as France won 2–0. Should have known better. In the afternoon Morocco played West Germany. I backed the Germans and, once again, it didn't look too good – until a last-minute goal came from Matthaus to win the game and my luck changed. It wasn't to last. The manager called a team meeting at 6.30 p.m. to name the subs and I wasn't among them. I suppose you could say there was some consolation after dinner when we had a race meeting at which Peter Shilton and I were the bookies. Shilts and I won £10 each out of six races, officially ending my losing streak, although it hardly made up for not being one of the substitutes.

The lads had nicknamed the Azteca 'The Palladium'. The view from the bench was restricted so Chris Waddle and I watched the game from an ITV commentary box behind the goal along with Manchester United's Ron Atkinson, Tottenham chairman Irving Scholar and Ray Wilkins. Following our 3–0 win Bobby Robson praised the players for their performance and gave us all a day off so we could have a few well-earned beers. There was also to be no prohibition on sunbathing, another big bonus. I backed Denmark later that day and they were duly walloped by Spain 5–1, with Emilio Butragueño bagging four to become joint top scorer with Lineker.

When we first arrived I'd been contacted by a local lad

named Fernando who was a Chelsea fan. A day off provided a good opportunity to meet him and he brought some friends and his mother. I gave him some memorabilia and he enjoyed collecting the team's autographs.

I was not on the team – or the bench – for the next match, against Argentina. By that point I think I knew that there was no realistic chance that Robson would change tactics. There had been a moment when I thought I might be out there, partnering Gary Lineker, but after Robson first opted for Peter Beardsley in support and the pair clicked, England had never looked back, certainly not back in my direction. My role, like everyone in the ground on the day of the Argentina game, would be to marvel at Diego Maradona. At least Shilts and I cleaned up as the bookies this time.

England v. Argentina at the Azteca was momentous, even at the time, and has gone on to be considered one of the iconic games in world football. I was proud to have been part of it, despite England losing to Argentina (well, to Maradona). The global focus on the game was particularly intense because it was the first encounter between the two countries since the Falklands War four years previously.

The atmosphere was something else, with a crowd of more than 110,000 creating giant Mexican waves – still a novelty – by standing up in sequence with arms in the air. What an atmosphere, what an arena, what an occasion, what a buzz... and I was once again stuck in an ITV commentary box behind the goal, along with Mark Hateley – once my rival for a starting place in the attack – goalkeeper Gary Bailey, Viv Anderson and Alvin Martin.

The game began with us filled with hope that England

would reach the semi-finals. By the end there was only one talking point and that was Maradona's 'hand of God' goal, one of the World Cup's most controversial moments. From my position in the stands at the far side of the ground behind the goal, I didn't have a clue that it was handball at first, as Maradona leapt in a blur that lasted a fraction of a second for the backward pass from Steve Hodge. It looped in the air as Peter Shilton went to punch it. Handball! I didn't see it but Mark Hateley was convinced. We peered at the TV monitor where the slow-motion playback showed conclusively it was indeed a handball. The controversy began immediately and with good reason. But I also look at it this way: if Lineker or Beardsley had punched in the winner, I don't think we would have complained so loudly, now would we? Yes, it was a form of cheating but there is an old saying in football, 'There is no such thing as a bad goal,' so how can I condemn Maradona? My overriding impression then was that he had scored one of the great goals. It was breathtaking. The dribble past half of our team lit up the whole competition. I was convinced I had watched the best player ever, better even than Pelé.

Maradona followed up minutes later with a goal of outrageous ingenuity and class, sheer genius, another contender for greatest ever. It was a privilege to have witnessed it. John Barnes and Chris Waddle were then brought on to give England width and they certainly scared Argentina, with Barnes beating his marker and providing a perfect cross for Lineker to pull one back, his sixth goal of the tournament, making him top scorer. I was really chuffed for Barnesy that he got to play as we had become very friendly while spending a lot of time in each other's company in the seven weeks of preparation. You could see that the Argentine defence was scared to death of him and for good reason.

John provided another cross, and Lineker thought he could equalise, only to be whacked in the back of the neck, a typical example of the tactics of a South American side when they are out to stop you scoring at all costs. Barnesy frequently provided crosses that were a striker's dream, but that last-minute chance was taken away by a clear foul. Without that I am convinced we would have gone on to beat them and reach the semi-finals.

We had done well despite the slow start and some setbacks in the early group games. The team had been evolving and improving, and it had some cracking good players in it. And as far as I was concerned, the longer we stayed in, the greater my chance of involvement, particularly if there was a knock or two among the front players. Right up to the last minute I had been convinced we could have progressed and that there might have been a role for me, maybe even in the final itself. You only have to remember how late in the day Geoff Hurst emerged in the England team of 1966. When Jimmy Greaves got himself injured, an opening appeared from nowhere and Hurst ended up scoring three, the first and only hat-trick to be scored in a World Cup final.

The mood in the dressing room after our defeat by Argentina was as you would have expected it to be; sombre and deeply depressed. We returned to our team hotel next to the Mexico City airport where Bobby Robson called us all together for one last team meeting. He thanked us all and told us that we had been a great squad both on and off the field, a credit to our country. We had worked terrifically hard, we had done our best. We all had a few beers that night, the manager joined us and so too did some of the football writers.

After we returned, I watched the final on television in Torquay, where I had gone for a few days' holiday, and saw how Diego carried Argentina as they beat West Germany 3–2.

I had played six minutes of World Cup football. Was it worth it? All that hard work to get into the squad in the first place, the heat, the time away. My answer is simple; it was worth it, even for those six minutes. Representing your country must be regarded as the highest honour for any sportsman and throughout the entire World Cup campaign, my only thought was that here I was one of the elite members of the England squad trying to win the cup. Ask how seasoned, top-class players like Trevor Francis, Tony Woodcock and Dave Watson felt when they were left out of the squad? I felt great sympathy for my Chelsea teammate David Speedie, promised a spot but left out by Scotland. George Best and my great idol, Ian Rush, the goal-scorer I admired more than any, never played in the World Cup Finals. I bet they would have swapped places with me. Just being there convinced me that I would become a better player, a better goal-scorer, and that I would be ready to be in the team for the World Cup in Italy in 1990.

You learn in this game all the time, and rubbing shoulders with the elite was a footballing education. Just observing the work rate and focus of a great goalkeeper like Peter Shilton was an eye-opener. The players believed he was the best in the world and he proved it in Mexico. Peter Reid's enthusiasm and commitment were remarkable, and Bryan Robson was a genuine world-class performer. As brave as any England lion, he refused to go home when injured and I'm sure that his namesake Bobby, was tempted to patch him up and send him out to mark Diego Maradona. Within two days of Bryan dislocating his shoulder he was out training with us. He never gave up.

The Mexico World Cup, though, was the making of Gary Lineker. Our paths had first crossed when Gary was in the Second Division with Leicester and my career was just beginning at Reading. I had attended, and Gary had been represented at, an Adidas award ceremony, both of us having won the Golden Shoe for being top scorers. Ever since I arrived in the First Division after signing for Chelsea, I was aware that Lineker was one of my great rivals for being the leading scorer but it was very much a friendly rivalry. Goal-scorers like Lineker and Rush cannot be stopped; they are goal machines.

But as much as I admired them, I wanted to be in the starting line-up for the World Cup in 1990. I took careful note of the change in emphasis in the team. No longer was my main challenger for No. 9 Mark Hateley. All eyes were on Lineker and Beardsley, the game was shifting and it was important for me to take that on board.

CHAPTER TEN

DRESSING-ROOM UNREST AT THE BRIDGE

The season following the heady experiences of the World Cup was a massive comedown in all respects. It seemed to be hardly at all about the football, and when I was playing my form was not great. It was a season I'd rather have forgotten in terms of playing, and in any case it was all but completely overshadowed by rumours about my future at the club. By the end of it I wasn't even sure I wanted to remain myself.

I first needed to talk with John Hollins and Ernie Walley to clear the air. Enough time had elapsed since the bitter disappointment of being left out of the final game of the last season for my anger to have subsided. But the hurt and embarrassment of discovering my omission from the team through the newspapers remained uppermost in my mind.

I wanted a full explanation. I had been able to give a great deal of time, thought and consideration to the unsatisfactory situation of the last months of the season. I knew that several top clubs were interested in signing me should Chelsea consider me to be surplus to requirements, but I had no desire to leave the Bridge. The club had been good to me, and my relationship with the supporters, who I rated as absolutely first-class, was fantastic.

As manager, John Hollins insisted my future was at Chelsea and that there was no way he wanted me to leave. He defended his decision to leave me out of the team for the final match at Watford, explaining that it would have been foolish of me to risk injury before the World Cup. He believed Chelsea's opportunity to win the League had diminished drastically because of my pelvic injury, alongside the unfortunate suspension of David Speedie. He was determined to avoid a repeat and had spent £400,000 on Gordon Durie so Chelsea could enjoy the luxury of choosing from four first-class strikers. I remained a highly valued member of the Hollins team, he insisted, and he wanted to make a more determined attempt at winning the title. My hurt and uncertainty were soothed away in our conversation, But almost immediately another huge row erupted from a completely different quarter.

Publishing an autobiography in 1986, when I was in my mid-twenties was, clearly, ill-advised, and including the punch-up with Speedo in the tale was an even worse mistake. A newspaper highlighted the story when *Kerry: The Autobiography* was serialised and made it seem much more than it was, with a sensational headline. Now I know more about the press, but at the time it came as a shock, and inevitably caused friction within our camp. Even before the new season had kicked off, things were kicking off inside the club.

The newspaper didn't include the vitally important qualifying sentence from my book: 'It seemed the clash between Speedie and myself was the best thing that could have happened as our relationship, both personally and professionally, blossomed from that point onwards.' All that the readers got to hear about was the argument and the very short fight. The key part – that we became great friends – was entirely omitted.

Both Speedie and Colin Lee, also mentioned in the incident, were startled by the newspaper report. Thankfully, having read the book, they accepted totally that the serialisation had taken the incident out of its full context. Nevertheless, I was disturbed that they had both been upset. Ken Bates was said to be delighted by the book, but nevertheless I was fined by the club. I didn't think the action was particularly fair at the time and, in truth, I still don't. But I felt it was best to accept the fine, if only to allow the publicity to die down. I was staggered, therefore, to read later in the season an onslaught by the chairman that suggested strongly that I was the cause of many of Chelsea's problems, because of the revelations about my punch-up with Speedie. I have always had the utmost respect for Bates, but his words hurt me deeply. I felt they were unfair.

David Speedie himself assured me that his own unrest at Chelsea had absolutely nothing to do with the newspaper serialisation. I remained convinced that the original punch-up had helped to forge the strong bond between us. In fact, it could be argued that it played a major part in Chelsea's rise from the Second Division. Few would have argued that our partnership was one of the most feared strike forces in football.

The season had begun badly and, sadly, gradually got worse, exacerbated by a great deal of dressing-room unrest. There was much speculation about John Hollins's future, which reached a climax when one of the newspapers ran a poll inviting readers to vote on whether or not he should be sacked. I had had my differences with the manager, but it was both unfair and ludicrous to suggest that all the troubles at Chelsea were down to him. Everybody at the club, from the chairman to the newest apprentice, was responsible.

Ken Bates did come out and publicly back Hollins. His support seemed to be unequivocal, but reading the gossip in the newspapers made it hard to sort out fact from fiction. And, understandably, our supporters could not comprehend how a team they had expected to challenge for the title could be struggling close to the bottom of the table. Relegation had become a distinct possibility.

Stories of player unrest were emblazoned across the sports pages, virtually on a daily basis. A series of transfer requests were exposed. Each player had, I'm sure, his own reasons. I was determined to keep my nose out of things. I had more than enough worries and doubts of my own to contend with. I was not scoring. My form at the start of the season had been reasonable but I needed a few successful strikes to get the adrenalin flowing and my confidence bolstered. I began to snatch at chances I would have put away normally without a second thought.

The first England game after the World Cup was in Sweden. I was named to play alongside John Barnes. There was much speculation that this was to be my last chance to show I was a player with international capabilities. It didn't help matters when Barnesy was injured after just six minutes and began limping badly. He was forced to pull out of the game at half-time. I received one chance in the entire match and I admit that I should have put it away without batting an eyelid, when instead I snatched and missed. We lost 1–0.

I was terribly disappointed to be left out of the next England squad but there was nothing I could do. I was not playing well for my club and consequently could hardly expect to hold down an England place.

I had not given up hope entirely that I could make it at international level. I had faith in the fact that Bobby Robson continued to watch me. But when he came to a game against Norwich in January 1987 it was the day Chelsea chose to drop me, and followed the press speculation about my relationship with the manager and my lack of form. It was all totally uninformed. John Hollins had kept me in the team when he would have had just cause in leaving me out. He kept faith with me during the first twenty-five games of the season, as if to demonstrate that, contrary to the popularly held suspicion, he did indeed rate me as a player.

When I was dropped against Norwich I didn't complain. He had given me a fair run when my form had not, perhaps, warranted it. Nevertheless, I suspect the press were anticipating a further demonstration of unrest at Chelsea with me asking for a transfer. The idea was a total non-starter. I was desperately disappointed, but I didn't question the motives behind the decision. John's job was to do what was right for the team, as well as what was right for me.

I'd had two years of almost non-stop football and I had not thought the involvement with England in the World Cup Finals would affect me. I was wrong. I hadn't had more than six minutes of actual playing in Mexico, but that time was preceded by two months of non-stop hard work and concentration. There had barely been a fortnight to spare between the end of the World Cup and the start of pre-season club training. I wasn't alone: several other England players also seemed to find it difficult to find their true form back home.

The problems I had suffered for much of the season came to a head when Chelsea made an abortive bid to buy Leicester's Alan Smith, who signed for Arsenal in March. Suddenly my mind was crystal-clear. I was focused on the situation that had been brewing for some time. There had never been a time when I had given less than one hundred per cent for Chelsea. But deep down inside I was unhappy with life at the club. I felt I had to get away, to make a fresh start. I had a feeling that Chelsea felt the same and that was why they had made the attempt on Smith. It had become impossible to produce that extra spark that allowed me to make my name in the game. I sat down and wrote my transfer request. One copy for the manager, and the other for the chairman.

I knew there would be a fuss when the request was made public but I hadn't been remotely prepared for the storm that followed. The fact that I was apparently the ninth player to ask to leave during the season added even more to the drama. One newspaper phoned to offer a staggering amount of money for me to attack certain people at Chelsea. I couldn't believe what was happening. There were so many false rumours; I threatened never to kick another ball for Chelsea; I would blow wide open all the secrets of the behind-the-scenes rows if my request was not granted.

I agreed to an interview with the *Mail on Sunday* in which I tried to explain the facts of the request. I spelled out the truth, that I needed new impetus. I said the decision to ask for a transfer was not made in the heat of the moment. It had been on my mind for a long time. I have never been a person to react in haste and then repent at leisure. The sparkle was not only missing from my game but the team was struggling. I'd been at the club for more than three years, which for the most part had been extremely happy. I remained deeply grateful to them for the opportunity they gave me when I was signed from Reading.

The game following my transfer request was an FA Cup tie at Watford on 1 February, one of the matches broadcast live on TV on a Sunday afternoon. I didn't really feel in the right frame of mind to take part in such an important game for Chelsea but I was named a substitute and, contrary to newspaper allegations that I wouldn't turn up, I was there on the bench.

I was booed heartily by Chelsea fans. I expected the treatment. Believe me, if I had actually said the words that had been attributed to me I would have booed myself. The supporters were hurt, and understandably so. The criticism would continue from some quarters until the end of the season. But as my form returned the vast majority of the fans got behind me again, for which I was truly grateful.

When I scored a couple of goals in a game against Leicester in May I knew the inevitable comparison would be made between myself and Alan Smith. In fact, he scored a very good goal and I was most impressed with his obvious ability. I was sure he would do well at Arsenal which, of course, he did.

At the end of our final game of the season against Liverpool I was invited by Chelsea to present a commemorative gift to the great Ian Rush, then playing his last game in a Liverpool shirt before his transfer to Juventus. It was a memorable moment for me because he was the master in our business of scoring goals. He had been able to maintain his fabulous record even though he knew all season that he was on his way to Italy in a £3 million deal. What a great player.

In contrast, I had equalled my worst-ever season as a professional with a return of just twelve goals. That represented an average of just one goal in almost four games. To me, it constituted failure. I had been so proud of my record of scoring one goal in every two games,

It would be difficult to re-establish that reputation, but even so I walked away from that season just glad it was all over. At times it had been a nightmare.

CHAPTER ELEVEN

TRANSFER RUMOURS

Ken Bates disappeared up the Amazon at the end of the 1986–7 season. He couldn't be contacted or didn't want to be disturbed and I was shocked to be told in his absence that both Arsenal and West Ham had agreed terms to buy me. It hit me that the club wanted me out of the door and that deals to sell me were being been done without my knowledge or approval. But that was the way business was conducted in those days.

Who actually wanted to get rid of me? It was a mystery. Was it Ken Bates? Was it John Hollins? It was hard to tell what precisely was going on behind the scenes at the Bridge, but it was a pretty turbulent time with the club never out of the headlines and rarely for its football.

Arsenal's interest had been rumoured for some time, but I never knew how true the stories were as no one at the club would ever discuss it with me. With so many articles appearing it was hardly worth asking the manager each time I saw a new one. Now it seemed it was really happening. I was told to speak to George Graham, the Arsenal manager and West Ham manager John Lyall. That came as quite a surprise to me, I can tell you. If two clubs were involved it was clear that Chelsea were determined to sell me.

It's hard to imagine the football dynamics of those days, a time when managers would meet players in discreet locations away from the prying eyes of supporters, the media and the like. These days there is no meeting in hotels off the motorway. Agents are far more active and powerful in discussing terms and players have no need to be dashing off for a secretive rendezvous with a potential new partner.

Assistant manager Theo Foley did Arsenal's groundwork and had brokered a deal that was virtually agreed by the time I met up with George Graham at a hotel off the M25. He asked me if the financial terms were okay and I told him that I was happy. It was actually less than what I was getting at Chelsea but not far off and looked like a decent move – if Chelsea no longer wanted me, that is. Arsenal certainly wanted me, there was no doubt about that and there was no doubt in my mind of the strength of their resolve. Graham told me his vision for the club and of his massive ambitions to win trophies. It was a tempting proposition, all right.

Arsenal planned to swap me with Niall Quinn and to pay £250,000 on top. West Ham, meanwhile, agreed a straight cash deal of £1.25 million. I met John Lyall and was also interested in the possibility of a move to Upton Park.

John Hollins said that the decision was ultimately mine.

The subtext was that my options did not include staying. I was being pointed towards the exit door. He spoke in the briefest and most abrupt terms, merely letting me know that the deals were on the table, although he did say again that he wanted me to stay. Ken Bates, meanwhile, was on his cruise up the Amazon and apparently out of contact. This didn't fill me with confidence that the chairman was keen for me to stay.

Hollins seemed naturally keen to give Gordon Durie, signed back in early 1986, a chance. Yet while he sometimes played all three of us as strikers I thought he was focused on breaking up the Speedie-Dixon strike partnership – and that was certainly the result. Speedo also had a turbulent relationship with Hollins and he was the first of the two of us to go, sold to Coventry in July 1987 to make way for Kevin 'Willo' Wilson, a good finisher.

I still wanted to remain at Chelsea. Nagging doubts remained at the back of my mind and I thought the only way to answer them was by confronting the chairman. Maybe he wanted to balance the books as the club had paid a lot of money for Durie. I decided to hang on to see Batesy when he finally came back from the Amazon. Surely he had to reappear some time? I would get my chance to thrash it out with him, to try to unravel the mystery. I wanted to hear from the chairman that Chelsea were going to let me go before I committed to either Arsenal or West Ham. I loved the club, I loved the fans, I had a special relationship with the supporters and I didn't want to relinquish that without knowing all the facts.

Finally, I got a message back from Bates. He told me to wait a couple of weeks before making any final decision and he agreed to speak with me on his return.

Meanwhile, the team continued to struggle and I wasn't the only one whose future was the subject of rumours. John Hollins was also the centre of gossip, much of which I ignored as far as possible, concentrating on my own patchy form. While we had a good team with some good players, we were not functioning properly together. The players were not gelling. Ernie Walley was also having difficulties as John's right hand man. Rows broke out between him, Eddie Niedzwiecki and Nigel Spackman. There was all round disharmony within the ranks.

The day after his return, the chairman called me to a meeting at his Beaconsfield farm. What happened at that meeting shocked me. Far from wanting me to go, he made it clear that he wanted me to stay and he was prepared to offer me a two year extension on my contract, which then had two years to run. I told him my preference was to stay and I accepted his offer there and then. A four year commitment! I wasn't expecting that.

Batesy asked me what I thought was going on with the team and what I thought was going wrong. I gave him my honest opinion. He made it clear that there would be changes and that I shouldn't worry about what had gone wrong under John Hollins and that I had every reason to stay. He said the proposals would be revealed in the next few weeks. This sounded to me like an intimation that he intended to get rid of the manager rather than me. This was John Hollins' first managerial position and it was clearly going wrong. But if there was friction between Ken Bates and John Hollins I didn't want it to be me who suffered by being forced out of the door. I had believed that managers were left to run the team and their decision on players, transfers and the like were theirs alone. It might have been naivety on my part but as a player I lived in a tiny bubble of training, playing, injuries and fitness, focusing on the game. These days I know that agents, benefactors, owners and their politics are working behind the scenes to influence what goes on in the club.

I now had the tricky job of contacting Arsenal and West Ham and telling them I had changed my mind. This wasn't going to be easy, as both clubs must have thought that I was about to leave Chelsea and join them. Theo Foley was most miffed, I could tell. 'So you're not coming to us after all,' he said when I broke the news to him I was signing a new, long-term contract with Chelsea. 'We were planning to build the whole team around you.' He took it badly at first but understood when I explained my feelings about Chelsea. As it turned out, they signed Alan Smith from Leicester instead and George Graham led them to the double. Maybe had I signed for Arsenal I might have gone on to my second World Cup in Italy. Who knows? But I have no regrets, because of my love for Chelsea.

John Lyall was a dignified man, a hugely respected manager of West Ham. We had me in a hotel room just off the M25 in South Mimms to discuss the transfer to Upton Park and, just like George Graham and Theo Foley, he had gone to great pains to sell the club to me. He explained that it was time for him to break up the Frank McAvennie-Tony Cottee partnership that had been so successful for the team. Frank was heading back to Scotland to play for Celtic while Tony was signing for Everton and he wanted me to come straight into their attack. Lyall was also understanding and respected my decision.

I felt vindicated in waiting to see the chairman. John Hollins had wanted to bring in Durie to the detriment of a strike partnership that had worked so well under John Neal and Ian McNeill and it was something I felt ultimately led to his downfall. John Neal had been one of the best – if not the best – of all the managers I had played under and it was sad that his heart attack curtailed his career. To be frank, the appointment of John Hollins hadn't worked out and I am sure even he would probably admit he had made a few mistakes. By March 1988 he had been sacked.

As a player I didn't really appreciate the intricacies of these decisions, how much they have to do with the politics of the game or the manager's true ability to galvanise a group of players, pick the right team and tactics and win football matches. It is a results-based industry but there is far more that goes on behind the scenes. Players didn't know for sure the relationship between John Hollins and Ken Bates and when and how the chairman had decided he wanted to change the manager.

Bobby Campbell had been brought in to assist John Hollins, but now he was appointed interim manager, effectively until the end of the season as we had eight games to go. But he couldn't prevent us from going down as the damage had been done by then and there was little he could do to remedy it in such a short space of time.

Off the pitch, matters were no more hopeful. Bates owned the club but not the pitch and was mired in a battle with property firms. Arguments raged over his Chelsea Village concept, with its planned hotels and entertainment venues. Yet there was little money to spare and Campbell had to use a hotel near the training ground as his office. The politics of the game went over my head and I just assumed that they wouldn't affect what was going on in the dressing room or on the field. Of course, events elsewhere in a club do in reality make an impact and it wasn't surprising there were so many turbulent years both off and on the field.

With Bobby Campbell in charge, the dressing room atmosphere changed. There had been a degree of confusion before, with John Hollins walking around saying one thing and Bobby Campbell saying another. I really didn't know who to listen to or who to talk to and I was never quite sure who had the final say on team selection. I wondered if the chairman was pulling the strings. I could ignore it for the most part as a player, but I guess it made a difference for John Hollins, particularly if he suspected he was for the chop. Now at least there was just one voice, although I'd still say that overall I had the best times at the Bridge when John Neal was the manager.

Even in the darkest hour, there was still a lot of light-hearted banter and fun in the team. I remember the lengths we would go to when we needed to hastily lower our weight to avoid a club fine. This would inevitably follow those times when we over-indulged at dinner – Wednesday was a favourite night of the week for this as it was the last day we were allowed out before the hard work really kicked in for the preparation for the Saturday game. We had to make sure we were in tip-top shape come the weigh-in at the Friday training session. Gordon Durie, Mickey Hazard and I would often put on a black bin-liner over our tracksuits while working out on an exercise bike in the sauna. Believe me, you can sweat out serious amounts of weight decked out like that. Then Thursday night would be beans-on-toast-night. Working to this schedule, I had no problem shedding the weight in time. I could sometimes drop as much as ten pounds in a session.

Glenn Hoddle once caught me undergoing this peculiar-looking routine. Bobby Campbell had invited him to come to the Bridge to help recuperate following a knee injury troubling him at Monaco. One day Glenn happened to catch me in the sauna going for it as fast as I could on an exercise bike, bin-liner in place, sweating buckets. He was amused and baffled in equal measure. 'What on Earth are you doing?' he asked. I don't think he'd seen anything like it.

The news elsewhere was unremittingly grim. Chelsea had climbed out of the Second Division in 1984 and now we were going to return. We had won just one of our last twenty-six fixtures of the campaign. We finished eighteenth in a twenty-one-team league, a position that would have been more than comfortable in other seasons. However, we were compelled to compete in promotion and relegation play-offs and, though we comfortably took care of Blackburn Rovers, both home and away, we narrowly lost the two-legged final 2–1 on aggregate to Middlesbrough at the end of May. We lost 2-0 in the first leg and Gordon Durie converted a Pat Nevin cross early in the second leg but another goal was not forthcoming, no matter how hard we tried. The volatile Chelsea supporters vented their anger and frustration and made a bad day even worse for the club.

That Chelsea team should never have got relegated. Gordon Durie and myself netted twenty-three times between us and we had started October second in the League! We only needed one win in the last few fixtures but instead we staggered our way through the matches with one draw after another, including one against champions-elect Liverpool and a damning 4–1 defeat at West Ham. We won only one of the last twenty-six matches, fourteen of which were draws, including a 3–3 and a 4–4. Eight of the final eleven fixtures ended in a share of the points, including a final home match against fellow-strugglers Charlton Athletic. A win would have avoided the dreaded play-offs and Gordon Durie's penalty gave us a half-time lead, but Charlton escaped when they equalised with twenty-five minutes remaining.

Although we had undeniably had two consecutive poor seasons we didn't deserve our fate and the play-offs were then modified so that a team in eighteenth position could never be relegated again. It had been a pilot that didn't work and we had paid the price. But it happened and that was tough to take. I was gutted, all the players were gutted, the fans were gutted.

But I didn't regret my decision to stay with the club. I didn't want to be thought of as deserting a sinking ship. I owed the fans much more than that and I felt it was time to repay them.

CHAPTER TWELVE

LIFE UNDER BOBBY CAMPBELL

I liked Bobby Campbell. I liked him as a manager and thought he was a great bloke, a really good person. He had faith in me, and he gave me confidence. He died in November 2015, while I was writing this book and though I attended his funeral in Knightsbridge, not far from our beloved Stamford Bridge, it's still hard to believe he's gone.

A Liverpudlian who turned out for Liverpool in his time, he enjoyed a wonderful career in football and fittingly he returned to Chelsea under Roman Abramovich, who had become a personal friend and valued Bobby's advice. I can fully understand why. Perhaps Bobby's passing contributed to the end of José Mourinho for a second time at the Bridge in December 2015, because I do wonder what advice he would have given the club's owner had he still been by his side. He was often spotted in Abramovich's executive box.

Campbell, initially in post on a temporary basis, was Chelsea manager between 1988 and 1991, overseeing our return to the First Division. When he was sacked and replaced by Ian Porterfield, Ken Bates took him on as his personal assistant, such was the affection in which he was held at our club. The turnout was amazing for his funeral, a fitting tribute to the man and the manager. From Harry Redknapp to Frank Lampard, the footballing family came to pay their last respects after he died of cancer at the age of seventy-eight .

It was a privilege to have played under him at Chelsea as we stormed back as Second Division champions, the only medal I actually won at the highest level of the game. It sounds incredible, but believe me I don't have any regrets about not moving to Arsenal when I had the chance. I could have gone on to sit on a pile of silverware and medals but I had a special rapport with the club and its the fans and it would have been a wrench to have left.

Campbell shared our ambition for a speedy return to the big time and swiftly pulled off a masterstroke in signing two wise old heads to steady the ship after the bitter disappointment of relegation. In addition to appointing Ian Porterfield as his assistant, Bobby brought in Graham Roberts and Peter Nicholas, who were not just influential on the field, but so important for morale and team spirit in the dressing room. Graham Roberts scored seventeen goals that season from centre-half, including thirteen penalties and Robbo was a great penalty-taker.

Over the summer, Campbell had sold star winger Pat Nevin, who had made so many goals for the strikers and continued to make a good case for me, Gordon Durie and other players such as Steve Clarke to stay with the club in the lower division. He also recruited goalkeeper David Beasant from Newcastle United, where he played for seven months. He had been at Wimbledon the previous year when they won the FA Cup and he became the first goalkeeper to save a penalty in a final. The win had been a huge shock for star-studded Liverpool. He had jumped at the chance to join us in our challenge to get back to the First Division in the same year. The fee paid by Bobby Campbell – £725,000 – was a club record but he was a good replacement for nervous youngster Roger Freestone. David immediately instilled confidence into a wavering defence. Bobby played me against fellow strikers Gordon Durie and Willo and Campbell and I thought it was a brilliant idea to use all three of us.

The campaign for our return actually started in the worst possible fashion, I was out injured and so too was Tony Dorigo when we were beaten 2–1 at home by Blackburn. We were not helped by the terraces being closed for the first six matches after crowd trouble. It took seven matches for our first victory to arrive, away at Leeds, but when we did start winning we continued on an amazing run, taking sixteen points out of eighteen. We were on our way back! We had a solid defence, marshalled by Roberts and it was this that provided the foundations from which our attacking players could make an impact and we all scored regularly up front.

We put four past Oldham and five past Plymouth, while Durie scored five goals in a 7–0 away win at Walsall. By February 1989, we were alongside Manchester City, both of us pulling away from the pack. By the time we met in

March, it was being billed as a title decider. It was a fantastic return to form for us. Thousands of Chelsea fans made the journey north for the game and it was a trip to remember as we produced a marvellous team performance, racing into a 3–0 lead. I scored, as did Wilson and there was a brilliant individual effort from Dorigo. The home side got two back towards the end of the game, but we held on for a victory that left us in a fantastic position.

We were unstoppable, in a run of twenty-seven unbeaten games. I scored four in a 5–3 home win against Barnsley and it was only a fortnight later that our streak came to an end with a 2–0 defeat away at Leicester. This proved to be nothing more than a minor blip, however and the following week we secured promotion – and the title – when John Bumstead scored the only goal of the game to beat Leeds at the Bridge, sparking jubilant scenes. On the final day of the season, Graeme Le Saux was given his debut as Kevin McAllister scored a brace in a 3–2 win at Portsmouth. We finished the campaign with ninety-nine points, a new record for the Second Division and finished a full seventeen points ahead of Manchester City.

My tally of twenty-six goals for the season was pretty good considering I had missed the first month of the season through injury, but the most important thing was that we were back in the First Division at our first go.

We opened the 1989 season with Bez getting an opening day opportunity to go back to his spiritual home, Plough Lane, as we beat the Dons by a single Kevin Wilson goal. Over the course of the season I hit twenty-six goals, helping us reach fifth by May 1990, our highest position since 1970.

To go from the Second Division to fifth in the First Division in the space of a year had been a remarkable effort. Campbell had shown himself to be adaptable, continuing to make room for the three forwards as well as playing a sweeper. By November we had climbed to the top of the First Division for the first time in decades and we made a promising start to our Full Members Cup campaign that same month. Alan Dickens scored a hat-trick as we overcame Bournemouth after extra time in the second round, eventually winning 3–2.

The format of the competition had been tweaked slightly from the last time we reached the final, in the wake of the post-Heysel ban on English clubs in Europe. Now there were straight knockout matches all the way through, rather than small leagues. The teams entering the competition were split into northern and southern sections, with the top side from each category meeting in the final.

In the third round we beat West Ham 4–3 at the Bridge just before Christmas. My goal and a Kevin Wilson brace then sealed a 3–2 win at Ipswich in January 1990 quarter-finals, setting up a two-legged semi-final against Crystal Palace. In the first leg, two goals in the space of three minutes – a volley from myself and a Wilson strike – put us in control of the tie and back at the Bridge we racked up a 2–0 victory.

The final was played in March at Wembley and we met Middlesbrough full of confidence after a 1–0 away win at Arsenal the previous week. We had started the match as favourites as Middlesbrough were in the Second Division. Our captain, Peter Nicholas, produced a brilliant last-ditch tackle to prevent Bernie Slaven from giving Boro the lead early on and Tony Dorigo curled a wonderful left-footed free kick into the top corner after twenty-six minutes, the only goal of the match, sending our fans into a frenzy at our victory.

In the last game of the season I scored a treble at Millwall – I had liked playing Millwall as I scored twice against the Lions at Stamford Bridge – and we won 3–1. My performance led to press speculation that I might be recalled to the England squad for the World Cup, Italia 90.

I had got a taste of playing in the cup in Mexico and I wanted to play again for my country more than anything. If there was even a glimmer of hope I wasn't going to give up. My club had enjoyed a good season, my goals were flowing again and it was in this frame of mind that I was phoned by the *Mail on Sunday*'s football reporter Joe Melling. He was very close to the England manager Bobby Robson and said I had a very good chance of a call-up. Joe told me I was neck-and-neck with another striker but Robson was seriously thinking it would end up being me. He thought I'd travelled well with the Mexico squad and kept myself in the general team spirit – not always the case when a player is not often used but remains part of the squad over a long, major tournament. The message was that the England manager felt he could trust me to be part of his squad. He knew what I was capable of doing. I was definitely in the shake-up.

However, to be fair to Robson, he never called me himself so perhaps I shouldn't have allowed my hopes to be raised as much as Joe's call did. I had no official communication from anyone at the FA yet when the squad announcement didn't include me, I was very disappointed. My final chance at another World Cup Finals had gone and Steve Bull was selected. But I harboured no feelings of bitterness or regret.

Maybe, had I signed for Arsenal or even West Ham, it would have been different, but that wasn't something that occupied my mind at the time.

Looking back now, I'd say I had a very good career at the highest level, scored a bagful of goals and come so tantalisingly close to becoming Chelsea's all-time leading goal-scorer. I do still wish I could have done more, done something a little better perhaps. I know that sounds like me expressing regrets, but that's not really the right word for it as I did have my chance to move on and I simply chose not to take it. I was, in the end, never sorry that I stayed on at the Bridge.

Perhaps I was unfortunate to have played in an era with so many outstanding scorers. Not only had Beardsley and Lineker formed a formidable partnership in the last World Cup, but there was a long string of potential back-up strikers that included Mark Hateley, Trevor Francis, Tony Woodcock and Paul Mariner and then there was also the new talent in the form of Mick Harford, Brian Stein, Ian Wright, Mark Bright, Paul Walsh, Tony Cottee, Clive Allen and Steve Bull, all prolific scorers with some of the biggest clubs.

I turned my focus back to my club and felt a steely determination to continue as Chelsea's top goal-scorer. The record set by Bobby Tampling of 202 goals was coming ever closer and I felt more able to reach it with every game.

For the 1990 season, Bobby Campbell brought in the club's first signings at more than £1 million, Dennis Wise and Andy Townsend and also began to blood youngsters such as Graeme Le Saux. I scored fifteen goals over the season, including a brace in a remarkable 6–4 win at Derby County and further League doubles against Everton (drew 2–2) and

Liverpool (won 4–2). Yet the season proved a disappointment and we finished at in eleventh place. Assistant manager Ian Porterfield took over as Bobby Campbell became Bates's PA. Eddie Niedswicki, who had suffered a knee injury, retired from playing to become one of the coaches under Porterfield.

Ian Porterfield's moment of glory as a player had come at Sunderland when he scored the winning goal over Leeds in the 1973 FA Cup final. When he coached us at Chelsea he was a popular figure and he went on to be manage Reading before returning to us as Campbell's successor. Other new arrivals included central defender Paul Elliott and midfielder Vinnie Jones, but there was no replacement when Gordon Durie left.

Porterfield had the foresight to try winger Graeme Le Saux at full-back, even though his suggestion was initially rejected by the player. Graeme wasn't the only one with strong opinions as Wise, Townsend and Jones made the dressing room a pretty lively place.

Vinnie Jones, in particular, was famously a figure you simply did not mess with. He towered over six foot at midfield, the ideal hard-tackling man in the middle, not afraid to dive into challenges and win the ball in the air. But it was said that he had a mean, aggressive streak; small wonder he was sent off twelve times in his career and he still holds the record for the fastest booking in English football after bringing down Sheffield United player Dane Whitehouse just three seconds from kick-off. Despite his lack of discipline, he made forty-two appearances in his solitary season at Stamford Bridge, scoring four goals. During that time I got to know a very different Vinnie Jones and came to like him a lot. He was vastly different off the field.

Vinnie was big and intimidating but little Dennis Wise was just as fearsome despite the height difference. Dennis was hugely popular and played alongside Vinnie in the centre of midfield in the 1991–2 season and was top scorer with fourteen goals. Dennis was fiery and had many run ins with the FA and opponents. Alex Ferguson once said that he could, 'start a fight in an empty house' and he was probably right. But he was amazing in many other ways as I came to know him at the club. He simply never slept. He was just too active and got up to all sorts of tricks. It was odd having him as a teammate and roommate as we all had detested him when he played for Wimbledon and we were often involved in brawls both on and off the pitch. Melees on the pitch often spilled over to pushing and shoving in the tunnel. They were the worst team to play against; constant intimidation, threats and nastiness.

Once at the Bridge there had been a twenty-three -man brawl after Dennis smashed Pat Nevin and sent the little fellow flying. They were both about the same size so it was quite funny really until we all piled in to have a go. Doug Rougvie was no shrinking violet and squared up to big John Fashanu as it all threatened to kick off during one game. They were face-to-face and the referee and two linesman were in there trying to separate the various player confrontations. But that was always Wimbledon's game-plan, it was all about physical intimidation and they had some truly big guys in their team, including Eric Young and Andy Thorn. We could never have expected that three members of the 'crazy gang' would end up with us at the Bridge. The many big personalities – with physical presences to match – on the team would have been a challenge to any manager, but particularly for a new boss such as Ian Porterfield, who had to deal with confrontation, arguments and internal strife.

After six matches, we were in second place but that was as good as it got. By the end of the season we had sunk to fourteenth . Still, along the way we stunned Liverpool 2–1 in February 1992 – our first win at Anfield in fifty-six years. Yet it was a disappointing season to close my time at Chelsea. But by then my playing was no longer the focal point that it had been for me. My personal life had gone totally out of control and a series of bad decisions and growing addictions forced me out of the club I loved so much.

CHAPTER THIRTEEN

THE ROAD TO RUIN

I had been called the golden boy of my generation at Stamford Bridge. The true picture of me out of the public eye was far less shiny. If I have any regrets, they aren't connected with my performance on the pitch; I was immensely proud of my record and how I conducted myself. But away from the game it was vastly different and I still rue the bad turns I took and the mistakes I made in life. The chaos I caused personally would eventually derail my career as a footballer.

My wages as a professional footballer were good for what players got in those days but I didn't keep hold of a single penny. It was all frittered away. I had the reverse of the Midas touch. Whatever I did turned to dust. Talk about a car crash of a life.

Whose fault was it? Mine. No one else's, just mine.

I started out in business for sound reasons; footballers

needed to look to the future, to the time they could no longer earn reasonable amounts kicking a football around and maybe even nothing at all from the game. There are only so many with the attributes to go into coaching and even fewer become pundits, certainly not the high-paid, elite pundits there are these days. It is never easy to find an alternative if all you have ever known is football and that was certainly the case with me.

I had been interested in the car rental industry ever since I'd had one as part of a sponsorship deal. Phil Podd had been the car-rental company's area manager and I knew him to be a genuine bloke, someone I could trust, so I decided to try my hand going into business with him. I was looking to safeguard my future and this looked like a decent opportunity. I was still playing at Chelsea when I took my first steps to becoming an entrepreneur. I wish I hadn't bothered.

I signed a £40,000 guarantee to lease a fleet. We had forty cars and the maintenance and various other bills were a total drain on my Chelsea wages. That would have been enough on its own but alongside it was my addiction to gambling. This was cutting far deeper than the betting sessions I'd enjoyed with the likes of the England squad in Mexico.

Now I can point as far back as thirteen as the age at which I became addicted to gambling, but, of course, I had no idea when I was younger that it was an obsession that would develop to be my downfall. As a teen at Challney secondary school, I used to play cards with a group of mates. The winnings were made up of our meal tickets, which cost 12p in those days (60p for a book of five tickets for the school week). If I lost I didn't usually go hungry as I would swap a ticket for a pudding, which my mates didn't generally eat. Some days, though, I had two tickets and there might even be a Friday when I ended up with five. I would trade them in the following week for more puddings. I had a sweet tooth and they were my favourite part of the school meal.

When a few of us were caught playing cards by a schoolmaster we were told to report to Mr Howells the sports master. I was the last in line outside his office. A lad called Eddie Woods – still a close pal of mine – was called in first and within minutes the word passed down the queue that he had been suspended from school. A similar fate befell everyone else before it was my turn to be confronted by the irate Mr Howells. It was then that I got my first taste of how my skill as a footballer might get me out of trouble and give me useful influence.

'I'm very surprised at you, Dixon,' said Mr Howells. 'You are the last boy I would have expected to be involved in something like this.'

He told me that he intended to telephone home and insisted I informed my dad what had occurred beforehand. I was dreading it. I returned home and duly broke the news. Dad was grim-faced but said nothing. After a lengthy telephone conversation with Mr Howells, he told me that I was to report to the sports master the following morning.

Mr Howells considered a caning or a period of suspension, similar to the punishment inflicted on all the other boys in the class, but decided against it because it would mean I would miss the cup final that the school team were proudly and anxiously looking forward to. He knew the school's best chance of winning was if I was free to lead the attack to score goals rather than be sitting in detention or suspended. He told me to join my class and be sure to score a hat-trick. Les Harriott my other good mate was also allowed to play, he was caught with us, it did seem a little unfair on the other hand.

We won the match 6–3 and I scored the hat-trick he had insisted on. This was the first inkling I had that being good at football allowed me to get away with things. It wasn't the kind of lesson I needed to learn at school and sent me the entirely wrong message. Maybe what I needed more than anything was a kick up the backside at that time. If I had missed the cup final perhaps I would have realised the consequences that might follow were I to continue down the road of becoming a fully fledged gambler. Being a football superstar could not be a shield against setbacks in life. This could have been a turning point but instead it failed to deter me from gambling – perhaps it even encouraged me.

Gambling is something that comes from a competitive nature and most footballers are highly competitive. I was exceptionally ambitious, even at an early age, determined to score and even more determined to be on the winning side.

By the time I had reached the peak of my career, gambling had become a disease that had taken a firm grip on my life. I'm convinced that it didn't affect my personality; I never allowed it to affect my football, but it might well be that I simply came to terms living with the disease because it became second nature. I really didn't think that I was hooked and I had no idea how tough it would be to break the addiction.

Betting on just about anything was in vogue, even in training. I once got into a wager at Chelsea with John McNaught, a central midfielder who thought he was quick enough to beat me over a sprint. I'm a big guy but I was much quicker than people gave me credit for; in fact, I was one of the fastest players at the club. John was formidably built, although not the most subtle of players and he was pretty cocky in training. Mickey Hazard set up the challenge and the loser was to pay a forfeit. None of us ever wanted to lose when other players were picking the penalty as it was usually something like having to do 100 press-ups or sit-ups. I gave John a head-start. While I stood on the touch line he took up a position on the edge of the eighteen-yard line. At the halfway point I passed him and by the end I was running backwards and he still couldn't catch me. It seemed like harmless fun and I couldn't see the darker side of gambling.

It is slowly becoming recognised that gambling is endemic in the dressing rooms at virtually every club in the country. Tony Adams was afflicted by alcoholism, but more recently publicly stated that the biggest problem inside football is gambling. He should know, having set up the Sporting Chance clinic to help others. Tony said that footballers have vast amounts of money to call upon now and even greater access to gambling without being detected through the internet. 'I think seventy per cent of our clients who come through as patients are gambling addicts.' Sporting Chance offers one-to-one counselling, residential treatment and education and training programmes

Drug use is also often mentioned but I didn't see any of that going on. Drug-testing is very efficient and I don't believe that footballers are interested in performance-enhancing substances. They might not even help performance as the game is as much about skill and finesse as fitness and power. If there is a drug that affects footballers it is gambling.

I'm not saying anyone I knew or played with were gambling addicts but plenty of the Chelsea players liked a bet. The strength of the urge to bet depended on each person's personality. I played in an era when the players loved a bet and a bevvy and I wasn't that keen on the booze.

I remember nipping down to Ascot one day with Steve Clarke, Gordon Durie and winger Kevin McAllister. We had had a very good tip that one of trainer Reg Hollinshead's horses was a sure-fire winner in the three-mile hurdle race. In those days heavy bets would affect the Tote and the odds fell after we all placed our bets from our box. All the lads won that day. I left Ascot with £35,000 in cash. One bookie had to close up, telling me he had lost £6,500 as a result of our big betting. I had been betting heavily myself, putting £100 or £200 on horses priced at 33s.

The betting didn't stop at the club, continuing seamlessly on England duty. In Mexico Bobby Robson allowed us a break from training to go to the races. Peter Shilton, Bryan Robson, Ray Wilkins and Kenny Samson were among the others who took up the offer. It was another Tote and when we bet on one particular horse from our box the odds started to tumble immediately. We started to place our bets on a horse at 6–1 and the odds were soon 4/6 favourite. I put my bet in but I don't know how much the others bet or indeed if they all placed a bet at all, but I assume that they did.

Back at Chelsea, it was common knowledge that I loved the horses. I used to go through the sports pages of every paper, particularly *Sporting Life*, to study the form. I was obsessed with keeping up with the runners and riders. Even on the team coach I had to have the racing on. Other players were into their own thing, reading or listening to music – Pat Nevin loved his music and would sit with his headphones on the whole journey. Nigel Spackman was the one with a video – but I was only interested in listening to the live racing. I used to sit at the front with the coach driver, Bruce Forbes and listen to the radio as there were plenty of times I could have as much as £3,000 on a particular race.

I got such a thrill out of betting and while I was over the moon if one of my horses came first, if I lost I wasn't down in the dumps as I could afford to bet big.

Bobby Campbell had to order me on the pitch to warm up as I was hanging back in the dressing room with a portable radio listening intently and waiting for a race to finish. I hurried out late having heard that I hadn't picked the winner, Chelsea won 4-3 and I scored a hat-trick so I probably should have put a bet on that! Betting clearly didn't affect my performance. Looking back I realise it was a way of life for me as the addiction took hold. When training was over each day I used to rush off to the bookies – I was faster getting away from the training ground than some of the nags I backed! We trained at Harlington near Heathrow and it was about a forty-minute drive home for me and then I was off to the local shop.

My agent arranged for me to make personal appearances and as a result of opening a betting shop I got an account with the bookie. This is the worst thing a gambler can do. Now I could put £200 and £300 on horses virtually every day without even having to go to the course or a shop. This changed the whole feel of gambling. When I put cash on the table at the bookies in person I got a good sense of how much I was spending, but it didn't seem as if I was using real money on account. I was just firing numbers down a phone. And these weren't trivial amounts. I thought nothing of putting £1,000 each way on this horse or that horse. Sometimes I won, often I lost – and I think a couple of the horses I bet on are still running... I just did it for the thrill, the high of betting. I once put £4,000 on a horse that didn't even run!

It was all too easy and convenient and I usually didn't have any idea of what the balance was. On one occasion a letter arrived from the betting account with a very long list of my transactions. Dad saw it and was totally shocked at the list of hundreds and hundreds of pounds going on races all the time. He couldn't believe it. He liked a little flutter once in a while, but coming from an ordinary, working background he just couldn't take in the amount of money I was throwing around and losing. He has not bet since. That made me stop, but only for a while.

The losses mounted up alarmingly quickly and I began to find myself in terrible trouble with bookies, to the extent that over the years I have lost a total of three homes. I bought a house in Edlesborough in Buckinghamshire, near Dunstable, for £70,000 when I started to make a good living out of professional football with Chelsea. It was a lovely cottage with some land and I spent more than £40,000 renovating the property. But I didn't really stay there that much and ended up re-mortgaging twice. Just two years after I purchased the place I had to sell it off for a knock-down price. I played football and gambled in a vicious circle in which all the money made from playing went into gambling and selling everything to pay off the mounting debts. I don't have a proper home now; I've nothing left.

When my gambling affected other people it made me feel really down and losing my home was a highly charged experience for me and my family. It affected Michele and Gemma and my parents to see me lose like that. They would ask why it was happening and where the money was going. The real answers were not easy for me. Invariably, I lied or didn't tell them the whole truth. I fobbed them off, expecting to keep on earning and to get back on my feet. It was a long time before the full story emerged. It was hard for me to accept my demons and even harder for those around me.

When Bobby Campbell was manager at Chelsea I was at one point £135,000 down and simply couldn't pay anywhere near it, despite my considerable earnings. At my peak at Chelsea I was earning £130,000 a year, something like £315,000 at today's prices. It was far away from what players earn today but still far many times more than what the vast majority of people were paid. And yet it was swamped by how much I was spending. I urgently needed bailing out and I went to Bobby for help. I was honest in explaining just how much I had been betting and how much I owed and he couldn't believe the sum.

'How did you get yourself in this sort of mess?' he said.

I didn't have an answer for him. I really didn't know myself.

But Bobby was brilliant. He said he would do something to help me out and he was true to his word. For that reason I must give him a special mention in this book. I appreciated what he did for me and I still owe him such a big thank-you. I only wish I had the opportunity to talk to him again, if only it were still possible. But I know he had a lot to do with the help I received from Ken Bates.

I'm guessing he went to the chairman and, whatever they decided to do, they sorted out some sort of deal. The bookies settled for £25,000 as a one-off payment and the club insisted that my account with them and all the other bookies were closed down so I couldn't rake up large debts again. How the club persuaded the bookies to accept a much reduced sum was never discussed and I have no idea to this day how it was done. I am sure Ken Bates would have the answers. All he said to me was a terse, 'The deal's done.'

The deal included me signing a new long term contract with Chelsea. It was never couched in such direct terms but I knew for sure that the contract was a trade-off for paying off my debts. I was happy to do so, even though I knew it was not on the terms I could have negotiated had I been starting from a position of strength. At that point I was just pleased to get the debt sorted.

Not only did my problem not end there but it was probably only a matter of weeks rather than months before debts began mounting up again. I just couldn't stop myself. It had taken over, I was out of control. But I still didn't quite appreciate that it was an addiction.

Ken Bates must have heard from someone that I was getting in deep again. Our paths often crossed in the corridors at the Bridge and on one occasion he just looked at me and said, 'Trouble again? When are you going to learn?'

It was a good question. As an obsessive gambler I always believed I could gamble my way out of my woes: I'll catch up on the losses... I'll make good... keep gambling, I'll win soon enough...

As my gambling debts mounted again, the bookies began

to send threatening messages. It always came through a third party but never directly from them. They were very plain in saying they would soon be dispatching the heavies to collect their debts. Jimmy 'the Wig' was a well-known character among certain footballers. He would be there to pass on messages if I asked him. Now he began talking to me, telling me to contact one bookie or another. 'It's getting serious,' he'd say. I got the gist.

Batesy dropped another little comment as we passed one another in the corridor one day.

'This can't go on forever,' he muttered, without stopping to talk.

Batesy was good for Chelsea and I liked him a lot so don't get me wrong if some of this sounds like I'm being critical. I'm not. Nor am I blaming him (Batesy – I love you really!). But he had a manner about him. Anyone who ever came into contact with him would know what I mean. You just knew when he had the hump and he clearly had the hump with me, I could tell, from his mannerisms and those little things he said to me in passing. He didn't need many words to get his message across. It was as much in the tone.

Let's be fair to the man, he had bailed me out once or at least he had seen to it that the club did so in some way. And yet he could see that here I was with still more debts. To be honest I would have liked the club to have bailed me out again, although I didn't ask them to. No one said anything, but it was reasonable to assume that Batesy was none too chuffed.

Bobby Campbell was also concerned about what I was getting into. He said, 'I don't know how you play football with all these problems. I don't know how you can put your mind into training and playing with all of this going on in your life.'

I can see why people might assume that my massive debts would have affected my playing, but to me it was normality. I just didn't take my problems onto the football field. If I was having a lean spell in scoring it was not because of any financial issues, not at all. My form was never linked to my gambling. Likewise, I never went through a run of scoring when I was winning. My personal life never entered my head, my thoughts were cleared of all that once I walked on the pitch and I was always totally focused on the game itself.

This was a way of life, it was my life. I bet and I collected a cheque or – far more often – I paid one. Certainly far more went out than came in. One week I would make a profit on one of my bookies' account and I would use that money to pay off a debt with another and then get extended credit with a third bookie. I regularly juggled one account with another, kept on gambling, kept on believing I'd win back my losses, but it never happened. I spent my time trying to keep one step ahead until, eventually, the debts caught up with me.

Sometimes I thought it was only happening to me, but I have since learned that Kenny Sansom has had his problems. I met up with him not so long ago and discussed the situation with him. Our stories with gambling are very similar. Other players such as Steve Claridge, Paul Merson, Keith Gillespie and Matthew Etherington have all voiced their experiences with gambling as a warning to others. They have talked very frankly about the problems gambling has caused in their lives, their marriages and relationships with loved ones and friends.

Matthew Etherington was an excellent winger with a

number of top clubs but has now come out to tell how he was gambling away thousands of pounds a week, ending up with £1.5 million of debt. Now retired from football, he says agents ask him to speak to players with gambling problems. A study conducted for the Professional Players' Federation in 2014 showed 6.1 per cent of sportsmen would be classed as problem gamblers compared with 1.9 per cent in the general population of young men. The research was based on confidential questionnaires from one hundred and seventy professional footballers and one hundred and seventy-six professional cricketers.

I think the true picture may be much worse and the problem may be more prevalent than players care to confess. I would say those figures could be very conservative. The vast majority of players want to keep their addiction to themselves and I can understand why. In the dressing room I would hear about it when someone won a few bob. Rarely did I hear them bragging about their big losses! If a player won one day in the week, it was likely they were suffering heavy losses the rest of the week but keeping quiet.

Yet it is good to talk about the problem. All of the players who have spoken out in public to explain their addiction and the horrendous effect it has had on their lives have said the experience has been positive. I hope that this book has that effect for me in the way that talking has done for those such as Paul Merson.

I have been to an addiction clinic in the past. Ken Bates sent me to one south-west of London that I was supposed to attend two days a week for a ten-week course. But it didn't seem to work after I'd been only three times and I stopped.

They dealt with all sorts of addictions with group sessions of about eighteen people, among them drug addicts, some dealing with abuse and violence. The clinic was known for doing wonderful things for some but it didn't help me. I found the experience quite harrowing. It wasn't anything like prison but nevertheless I was a 'face'. I found the stories behind different addictions were very similar and I could see the desperation of people wanting to escape the issues ruining their lives.

The work included explaining to the group why and how I became a gambling addict. I also had to describe situations that I would have to deal with and the following week report back about how I was coping. I quickly stopped gambling, decided I didn't need the sessions but soon drifted back to betting. Today, I believe that those who cannot control gambling do need to seek help and that is something I am now contemplating again myself. That said, I have better will power now and usually have so little money (often none) that on the rare occasions I do bet, it's more likely to be £1 or £2. Betting is always inside me, it will never disappear, but I think the question is more about how I control it than being about eliminating gambling entirely. It's not easy, no one can pretend that it is, so I am not going to try, but I feel I have it under control. If there are lapses and there will always be lapses, I hope there will be fewer.

The biggest problem remains the stopping and starting. I have quit on numerous occasions, only to get sucked back in again. But usually when I tell myself to stop I can do it. I am now more determined than ever not to go back to those dark days of unrelenting debts. I don't have any accounts with bookies, I don't have credit and now I only have cash to play with I know I cannot afford to lose it. I am no longer able to create that distance by ringing the bookie.

My mum and dad have been brilliant. They have bailed me out a few times and I don't want to let them down any more. 'Most roads end in nought'. That is the truth about gambling. All I can say in my defence is it led to financial ruin, and it was self-inflicted. I didn't mean to harm anyone else, and I'm sorry if along the way you are one of those it did, it is something I regret greatly.

I must underline again that the gambling had no effect on my ability as a footballer and a goal-scorer. I passionately believe that to be true. I bet when I played for my club. I bet when I went to the World Cup in Mexico with England. I bet all my life. But I continued to score goals on a regular basis for Chelsea as indeed I scored for my country.

CHAPTER FOURTEEN

LEAVING THE BRIDGE

Despite the problems I was increasingly having with gambling, the background to my departure from the Bridge remains clouded in mystery. I've not truly got to the bottom of why I was forced out.

I loved every minute of my time at Stamford Bridge and couldn't believe it recently after José Mourinho was sacked in 2015 and a fan's tweet suggested that the 'real Chelsea' was back in the 'days of Dixon and Speedie'. It was great to still be remembered in those terms.

I had no regrets about not joining Arsenal, no regrets that it was suggested I might have gone to Manchester United and no regrets I didn't make it to my second World Cup Finals. I was delighted to have been a Chelsea player for nine years and generally I don't look back with regret on any aspect of my time there; far from it. I had good cause to think I had a very good, if not outstanding, career with the club. That's not entirely true – if I have one big regret it's that I was not there long enough to break Bobby Tambling's all-time scoring record. I left within touching distance (one hundred and ninety-three to his two hundred and two), having recorded more than Roy Bentley, Peter Osgood and Jimmy Greaves. Who knows, might I have gone on and scored so many goals that even Frank Lampard couldn't have beaten me (he overtook Tambling in 2013)?

I managed to net only six in the 1991–2 season, when we finished mid-table, but overall I wasn't too concerned at my performance. There were reasons for it, as there always are when a striker hits a lean spell and I never thought for one minute that I couldn't get the goals again in a high enough quantity to justify my place.

It was true that our last serious chance of a major trophy had come the previous year, when we went on a good run in the League Cup but lost to Sheffield Wednesday in the semi-finals and it was also true that what turned out to be my final season was a low point in terms of goals by contrast with the number I usually recorded. In 1990–1, I scored what I thought was a credible fifteen goals, including doubles against Derby County (6–4 Chelsea win), Everton (2–2 draw) and Liverpool (4–2 Chelsea win). We ended up mid-table that year too.

My final goal, as it turned out, for the Blues was against Norwich City in March 1992. At the time I didn't know it was the end and although we won 1–0 it's not the way I would have wanted my career at Chelsea to finish. At least I went out with a bang, a spectacular shot from the edge of the box, a lovely winner.

Departure certainly wasn't on my mind at the end of the season when we went on tour to Canada. Why Canada? I've no idea. Perhaps money was offered to the club but it was sold to us as a lovely bonding trip for the players and, boy, did we know how to 'bond' in those days. We managed a couple of games – a draw and a win, I seem to remember – but it was the bonding with little training to distract us that made it more like an end-of-season holiday than a tour. Yes, plenty of beer, but that was par for the course. I wasn't the biggest boozer, but I did my best to keep up the pace.

The highlight of the trip was the visit to the Whistler Maritime Resort, where we experienced white-water rafting for the first time. We all went in our t-shirts while there was snow on the peaks. It was still pretty hot where we were. Four to a dinghy, among us Dennis Wise, Steve Clarke, Vinnie Jones, Tony Cascarino, and everyone in crash helmets. We had a paddle each and buckets to bail out the water. I concentrated on my task of making sure we didn't capsize using my bucket to bail out loads of water, in what turned out to be our toughest training session by far!

One morning on the Canadian trip I met Ken Bates for breakfast. He told me that the club were investing in two new strikers costing more than £2 million, an awful lot of money to splash on players in those days, an awful lot and the inference was that he was looking to balance the books. There was a chance that there would be sales and the subtext was that I would be among them. I had negotiated a new contract in return for Bates agreeing to sort out my debts from gambling and failed businesses and I had three and a half years left. I didn't have to move if I didn't want to. And

I didn't want to move. I was in sight of Bobby Tambling's record and I felt highly motivated about the new season with my aim of becoming the club's all-time greatest goal-scorer.

But Bates made it pretty plain to me that it might very well be in my best interests to move on and that I would be spending the next three season in the reserves without a sniff of a first-team place. That sounded pretty brutal to me and somehow a touch strange. I wasn't quite over the hill and managers need reasonably big squads to cover for injuries or suspensions. It took a while for what was being said and what was being hinted at to sink in and left me with a rather odd feeling that I was being pushed out.

In all honesty, a lot of what went on behind the scenes that summer still isn't totally clear to me. I have my suspicions about the political intrigue that was about to result in my departure from the club at a time when I still thought I had goals left in me and plenty of them. I would guess that the club disagreed and thought I was in decline. I also suspect I had given them enough trouble in the past, particularly as far as the dictatorial Ken Bates was concerned. He was probably right to be concerned about me because of my gambling and failed business ventures and I guess he thought that this was the time to bring in new strikers.

Bates didn't tell me who they were buying. Maybe he didn't know at that time and had a list of options. If I had discovered then who the club was going to recruit I might have had second thoughts about leaving, but by the time I knew it would be too late. They got in Mick Harford, who did all right for them and Robert Fleck, who didn't have the best of times. It didn't really matter. Whether it was my lack of goals, my debts or something else, the result was the same. Bates made it clear to me I'd be better off leaving.

Bates said, 'We are buying two new strikers for £2 million. I cannot see you playing in team. I would get in touch with your agent Brian Roach and start finding yourself a new club.' That was it, nothing else, Bates is a man of few words but he doesn't mince them when it comes to business and he left me in no doubt. My opinion wasn't requested and there was little point giving it.

The point remained that the club couldn't get rid of me if I didn't want to go as I had that long contract. I went to see Ian Porterfield and he told me that he didn't want to get rid of me! That only added to the intrigue. You would think that the chairman would have discussed such an important matter with his manager. If the manager wanted me to stay, I reasoned, then it must be the chairman who reached the decision about my future.

A week later Porterfield told me that Southampton had made an approach. Manager Ian Branfoot wanted to reach agreement with me about a move to the south coast club. As Chelsea had not officially transfer-listed me it was obvious they had been touting me around behind the scenes.

Porterfield said, 'If I said, "Kerry, I don't want you to go..."' Well, that took me by surprise, as at that point I still thought that chairman and manager were acting as one and, in fact, that the driving force behind all of this was that a manager agitating for change had lost faith in me. It seemed as if he wanted me to stay, to fight for my place and I realised he must have been fully aware of which players the club were about to sign. In hindsight, I should have held my nerve. I know I would have won my place back, I would have gone on to beat Bobby Tambling's record and I would have scored an awful lot more goals in the next few years.

The ongoing financial problems I was suffering made it that much harder to continue battling even if I'd been determined to do so. Alongside my gambling debts were rising costs from the failing car hire business. I had signed a £40,000 personal guarantee and a joint agreement with my partner that effectively amounted to a £40,000 overdraft used to pay overheads, staff wages and maintenance. Now my partner stood to lose his home and I couldn't allow that to happen as he was a decent bloke. It wasn't his fault it all went belly-up. The nature of the joint agreement meant that one or other of us would have to pay the £40,000 and sue the other one to get their money back. I decided that I would pay it off to save my business partner but I didn't have the heart to sue him to get my money back. I left it and moved on in my life. And moving on meant being sold to Southampton for £575,000.

My accumulated debts were to be paid out of my new contract, so it was a problem solved overnight by moving to the south coast club. In the end it wasn't so much a tempting move as one that I had no option but to take. In addition, I received signing-on fees from Chelsea as part of the previous contract as well as from Southampton. An awful lot of money came in, but it went out just as quickly. I paid off the Allied Irish Bank, who were threatening me with a High Court writ. It was worth it as I hadn't wanted to arrive at the gates of my new club embroiled in legal matters.

The greatest tragedy was that not long afterwards my car hire business partner Phil died of a brain haemorrhage. I have no doubt that he suffered stress as a result of the company going pear-shaped. We had been close and he had become a friend of the family. We went on holidays with his wife Ginny and two children Matthew and David.

Looking back on that time, I don't think I could have changed things, even the many bad decisions I made. It just wasn't possible. The way I behaved was in my DNA. And at the end of it, at least I had avoided bankruptcy.

Much later I would find out that Ken Bates had fond memories of my nine years with the club. When I had my testimonial at Chelsea, he wrote in the souvenir programme, 'Bobby Campbell told Kerry he was too good-looking to be a great centre-forward. He had all his own teeth, his nose was its original shape, there were no marks on his flawless skin. But irrespective of all that, Kerry finished up with 193 goals. He was never sent off, was rarely booked and was a total good sport in the real meaning of the words... For me, Kerry, you'll always be the Golden Boy of Chelsea.'

John Neal, one of the managers I respected the most of all, wrote: 'Such power. He was a great mover. The supporters loved him, he was a hero in the Shed and he gave everyone great entertainment. But I was lucky. I didn't just see him in games, I coached him. I saw him down the training ground every day. I think we got our £150,000 worth there... Within two years, Speedie and Dixon were on a par with Rush and Dalglish at Liverpool, and probably scoring more goals. What a lovely sight, Kerry in full flow. A beautiful sight. Very nearly the best in the country, if not the best... Kerry was just a smashing lad. I had all the time in the world for him. He always did everything you asked."

Gary Lineker had his say too and I valued his contribution. 'I first remember hearing of him at Reading, but at Chelsea he quickly became part of a successful team and partnership with David Speedie and was obviously very popular at the club. We played together for England and he scored some good goals and I got to know him then. He was a nice guy, typical striker, lived to score goals. For two or three years we were always fighting to be top scorer and we shared the Golden Boot in my last season at Leicester. I was very pleased that they gave us one each, so we didn't have to cut it in half.'

Dennis Wise had his say (I'm not sure about the nickname): 'When we used to go on away trips he would have the biggest suit carrier of anybody. It had all his awful gear in it. The tie would be one colour, the jacket another, the trousers a third. Nothing matches. Everything was just thrown in. Then there were all his wigs. "Kel" was more worried about his hair than anything else. Not many people know this but he had more hair on his chest than on his head. I know because I was his room partner. We were Little and Large. He was a good room partner.

'We always had a good laugh. No one messed about with us. They didn't dare, not after a couple of young lads tried it once. It was Damian and Jason and when we found out we made sure that no one would ever try it again. I'm afraid it's unprintable what we did on that occasion! It was great playing with "the wig". I enjoyed every minute, as a player and as a friend. It's a pity he didn't go on just a bit longer because I'm sure he'd have broken Bobby Tambling's record.'

And so I left Chelsea in 1992 and joined Southampton, where I briefly linked up with David Speedie again, though not with the same success.

CHAPTER FIFTEEN

SOUTHAMPTON TO MILLWALL

Southampton bought me from Chelsea to replace Alan Shearer, following his 1991–2 season at the Dell. With Southampton under new manager Ian Branfoot, Alan left for Blackburn Rovers as the club's leading scorer with twenty-one goals, having played a staggering sixty games. Blackburn had just gained promotion under Kenny Dalglish and Alan joined them in a deal that involved my old partner David Speedie coming to join me at Southampton, to the disappointment of Blackburn fans who had seen Speedo score the goals that got them into the newly created Premier League. But it had been the prospect of teaming up with Speedo again that had been one of the things that enthused me about Southampton.

Ian Branfoot brought in a number of players, including Perry Groves, who had helped Arsenal win the League Championship in 1988–9 and 1990–1. Iain Dowie was another signing, bought from West Ham for £530,000 and they became very good friends of mine. Unfortunately, all the chopping and changing at Southampton led to a them-and-us syndrome between the arrivals and the established players at the Dell.

Speedo hadn't changed much and, let's be fair, no one really expected that he would. As at Chelsea he had a fiery relationship with the manager and matters inevitably came to a head. He wasn't happy with the style of play and Speedo being Speedo he voiced his feelings in no uncertain terms. Ian Branfoot thought maybe we all needed a change of scenery and took us to the Isle of Wright for a midweek bonding session. In one of the rooms at the front of the Grand hotel, Speedo and Terry Hurlock had an altercation that quickly got out of hand and grabbed the attention of all the players; some bonding trip. Micky Adams, Glen Cockerill and Steve Wood dived in to separate them. As the fight was breaking up, Terry picked up a glass ashtray from one of the tables and hurled it at Speedo (who ducked), hitting Micky Adams on the side of the head. There was blood everywhere. The police were called and Speedo and Terry spent the night in the nick. Ian Branfoot was not amused and instead of training the next morning, the manager ordered us all to take a walk along the beach to cool down. Speedo was ordered home and never appeared for the club again.

Terry Hurlock, like Speedo, became a friend of mine, although both came with fearsome reputations. Intimidating and long-haired, Hurlock could be found in most top lists of hard men of English football, whether through his time at Brentford, Reading, Millwall, Rangers, Fulham or the Saints. Well, with seven red cards he was one of the game's biggest sinners! He had a no-nonsense and combative style and often got into scrapes off the field as well as on it. Hurlock and Speedo made a volatile combination. Yet neither were as they were portrayed in the press, even if they did live up to it on the Isle of Wright.

Speedo was becoming one of my best friends and it had been good to be back in the same team as him – albeit briefly, until that temperamental part of his character led to a parting of the ways for him and Southampton. Our partnership had hardly got a chance to get off the ground before he was off. On the field I rated him as one of the great footballers of his time and certainly he and I had forged a truly great strike partnership during our time at Chelsea. We complemented each other's skills and that was what had made us ideally suited to be a pair.

My stay at Southampton was not much more productive than Speedo's. I only made nine league appearances and two goals, with a total of twelve games in the seven months I was on the south coast. Needless to say, I was not considered a huge success! But, to be fair, I was injured for most of the time, including three months out with a back injury. After that I was in and out of the side and clearly nowhere near as fit as I needed to be.

Ian Branfoot called me in one day and told me that Luton's manager David Pleat wanted me on loan. Southampton had agreed to let me go. It was great news, just what I wanted to hear. It hadn't worked out very well for me down on the south coast and here was the opportunity to play for my home-town club, where all my mates came from. Luton was the place in which I had wanted to make my mark all those years ago. Once, David Pleat and Luton had showed me the door

– kicked me out – and now, all these years later, they wanted me to play again. The same manager who let me go wanted me back, I could hardly believe it. I was so overjoyed at the prospect.

I left Southampton in February 1993 to join Luton, initially on loan, with the move being a free transfer. It was made permanent in October. My first game for Luton filled me with the most wonderful feeling, playing in front of home-town fans at the club I supported as a boy.

David Pleat had put together a decent enough team that included the emerging John Hartson, over six foot and seventeen years old at the time. Pleat told me that my presence at the club would help to nurture the young talent. I partnered Phil Gray, a Northern Ireland international, up front.

I ended up staying two and a half years, extending my career in what was the old Division Two and was later known as the Championship. My roommate on away games was David Preece, who became one of my best friends. A left-footed midfielder, Preccy helped Luton reach two Cup Finals and an FA Cup semi-final and more than earned his place in the club's hall of fame. He began his career with Walsall before moving on to Luton where he made 395 appearances and was part of their 1988 League Cup winning team. He also had spells at Derby, Swindon, Birmingham, Cambridge and Torquay. I knew his whole family and we both lived in the same area. He was a gambler but he was much more sensible and reserved than me. All round he was a top man. It was a terrible shock when he died at the age of forty-four, in 2007, from throat cancer. Roy McFarland, who Preccy assisted at Cambridge, read a lovely speech. To die at such a young age was a terrible tragedy and I thought that McFarland was very moving in his tribute.

The highlight of my time at Luton was a thrilling FA Cup run. David Pleat liked attacking football and that suited my style down to the ground. He had a wonderful team that included really good players such as Scott Oakes, the key player in that cup campaign, John Hartson and Des Linton. Pleat prided himself on the fact that we cost, collectively in the transfer market, the least of any First Division side. We had a terrific streak that included a great Tony Thorpe goal getting us a draw at Newcastle, with John Hartson and Scott Oakes scoring to beat them 2–0 in the replay at Kenilworth Road. In the quarter finals we faced West Ham in a match that ended 0–0. Then the draw for the next round was made and the numbers that came out of the little black box at the FA pitched us against my old club Chelsea – if we won the replay, of course.

The night of the replay in March 1994, the band Showaddywaddy were playing up the road in Milton Keynes. Their guitarist, Trevor Oakes, was the father of Scott but that day it was his son who was the star of the show. We went 2–1 down – our goal coming from Oakes, then aged twenty-one– and recovered to win 3–2 after Oakes completed a hat-trick for which I made two. No one could possibly have been more pleased than me. Oakes persuaded the linesman to give him the match ball afterwards, got me to sign it and I joked, 'You have made an old man very happy.'

The team prepared for the semi-finals on 9 April 1994 and I prepared to face Chelsea for what I hoped would be one of the most sensational matches of my entire career. No one could have been more on edge, more anxious to do well. Unfortunately, we didn't perform as we knew we could and we didn't do ourselves justice. It was not a great game, either. We lost 2–0, with Gavin Peacock getting both goals. I had so much wanted to get to the FA Cup Final as I knew it would be my last chance, but if nothing else I had hoped that at least I would get on the score sheet.

At the end of the match, Dennis Wise put his arm around me and said Luton had been unlucky, but what moved me the most then and will live with me forever was the reaction of the fans. Chelsea's 40,000 supporters broke off from their celebrations to chant, 'There's only one Kerry Dixon.' It was a heart-warming moment, a highlight of my career in terms of pure emotion. Their spontaneous gesture made that decision not to sign for Arsenal or West Ham all the more worthwhile. Here was the proof that I did have a special affinity with the fans.

Their reaction meant more to me than the testimonial I received at Stamford Bridge a year later. It was held on 27 March 1995, four days after I was transferred from Luton to Millwall and, to be honest, it wasn't much to write home about. It snowed that night and the crowd attendance was disappointing, even though it was a reasonably attractive game against Spurs. I scored the first goal in an enjoyable evening and I was grateful to everyone who helped me to stage it. But after everyone dipped in to take their expenses for putting on the game I was left with around £50,000, far less than I had been hoping to raise.

Testimonials today are completely different. The top players are happy to hand over the takings to charity and quite rightly so, when some of them are earning £200,000 a week or more. But back then the money went to the player because he needed it – at least, I certainly did. No one knew how badly I had fallen on hard times and I am sure they wouldn't have sympathised even if they did. I'd had enough chances in my life and I squandered them. I still had gambling debts I needed to pay off, more business failures and also had to look after my family, with three children to care for. I was on a treadmill of debt, but I'd made it myself and there was no one else to blame but myself. If the supporters knew how I'd wasted my money, maybe there might have been a few less turning out.

I had to prolong my playing career because I needed the money but despite the debts that wasn't the only reason I continued. I hadn't fallen out of love with the game and simply wanted to carry on as long as I could. In all I scored twenty goals in eighty-eight appearances for Luton and enjoyed every minute of it, but I moved on to Millwall willingly at the age of thirty-three. David Pleat, who had been such an excellent manager during my time at the club as well as a good bloke, called me in to say I had done well for him and for the club, but it was time to let me go. He was doing me a favour as he knew I wanted to continue competing. I could hardly complain because he had signed me seventeen years after letting me go as a kid and I was grateful for that second chance at my home-town club. I had fulfilled my childhood dream of playing at Kenilworth Road and Pleat and I have remained friends. He was one of those who cared, both when I was a player and later when I hit rock bottom.

I joined Millwall in a £5,000 transfer deal with Mick McCarthy and was on loan to the end of the season. I didn't have an easy time at the Den. During my first game on twenty-five March at home against Tranmere Rovers, the Millwall fans chanted 'Scummer!' Not a great start with the home support, to say the least. The fans knew I had played for Chelsea, something of a red rag to Millwall supporters, but this was the insult that Southampton and Portsmouth fans flung at each other, for the fans also knew I had played for Southampton. Apparently, the original meaning of 'scummer' was 'a person who attacks and robs ships at seas: a pirate'. I never quite saw myself as a pirate. Then I scored in what was a 2-1 win and suddenly the fans changed their opinion. In fact, as it turned out, I went on to have a wonderful time at Millwall. Mick McCarthy felt I had done well enough to keep me on for the following season and I was delighted to sign a one-year contract.

During my time we had some really good players, including Ben Thatcher, Kenny Cunningham, Keith Stevens, Chris Malkin and Kasey Keller, yet we went down in 1996. Millwall fans are split in two over the blame for the relegation that cast a shadow over McCarthy's reign, despite it happening three months after he left. In early February 1996, we were in ninth place in the division, five points off a promotion place, outside the playoff zone on goal difference and a comfortable fourteen points clear of the relegation zone. It's often argued that we had been in such a slump in December, where we lost five straight games, that relegation was a certainty. Others put the blame firmly at new manager Jimmy Nicholl's feet and say that under McCarthy we'd never have gone down.

By that time I had already left the club myself. I made thirty-one appearances, seven of them as substitute and scored nine goals, before being sold to Watford for £25,000 in January. Manager Glenn Roeder offered me a two-year contract, which was the main attraction. I was focused on keeping my career going as long as possible and didn't take anything else into consideration. I was a complete fool not to have done my research or I would have discovered the manager might get the chop any day and realised just how much the fans were opposed to my arrival. Luton and Watford were local rivals and the supporters were hardly going to welcome a Luton boy with open arms. In fact, Watford fans mounted a protest against my signing for their club! Now that doesn't happen very often.

Roeder was duly sacked within two games of my arrival – leaving me without an important source of support – and back came Graham Taylor. The former England manager was a Watford legend and little wonder, he deserved to be after what he achieved as manager there the first time. Graham also brought back Luther Blissett as his second-in-command, another Watford hero, who scored plenty of goals for the club in his heyday.

Taylor told me that he was more than prepared to give me a chance, but in reality he used me only fleetingly and I wasn't in the team every week. He made it clear that if I got an opportunity to move on then I should take it. I didn't resent his approach to managing me; it was a fair comment at this stage of my career. I would always rather know exactly where I stood than be left wondering about what was going on behind the scenes.

Having signed a two-year contract, I knew I could sit on it and keep drawing my wages, but I still wanted to play the game on a regular basis. As it was I appeared in eleven matches for Watford without scoring a single goal before an opportunity came along to move into management with Doncaster Rovers.

CHAPTER SIXTEEN

CLASHING WITH VINNIE

I made many friends in my years as a player and some remain close to this day.

Vinnie Jones became a firm friend when he spent a season at Stamford Bridge. His footballing career began in 1984 when he was nineteen and, much as I did to begin with, he combined it with a regular job, working as a hod carrier on building sites. Vinnie was a defensive midfielder who was especially noted for his very aggressive style of play, and he made the most of his tough-man image.

He is now known as an actor, often playing violent criminals and thugs. His 1998 film debut was Guy Ritchie's cult gangster flick, *Lock, Stock and Two Smoking Barrels*. He co-starred alongside Sylvester Stallone and Arnold Schwarzenegger in the thriller *Escape Plan*, released in 2013.

For me, he was nothing like his reputation. The public have

one view of Vinnie but when I got to know him, I quickly discovered he was completely different in private, at least for the vast majority of the time!

Vinnie was sent off twelve times in his career and held the record for the quickest ever booking in a football match (three seconds for a foul on Dane Whitehouse between Chelsea and Sheffield United in 1992). He wrote of the incident in his autobiography: 'I must have been too high, too wild, too strong or too early because, after three seconds, I could hardly have been too bloody late!' He has a wicked sense of humour, a great sense of fun and I immediately took to him.

He arrived at Chelsea in 1992 the year I left. He didn't stay long, but when I finally got enough money to buy a house again, I decided I wanted to celebrate. It had been a long time coming so I threw a house party when I moved into the new place in Toddington. I mainly invited my mates from Chelsea and Luton, as well as my personal friends from the Luton area. One of my mates who played for both Spurs and Luton, Mitchell Thomas, had a big falling-out with Vinnie, who head-butted him. I hadn't a clue what it was all about, but whatever it was, Vinnie was bang out of order and I let him know exactly what I thought of him over the incident. But he was clearly still very angry and said, 'Don't invite me to any more of your f***ing parties.'

He was right in my face and extremely aggressive. I ended up punching him and Vinnie went down. There was a bit of a melee with Vinnie's mates, as pushing and shoving spilled into the garden with more blows exchanged. I told him to leave.

His mates rushed off and got his car and Vinnie departed,

shouting and threatening as he went. I didn't take him seriously. There wasn't much discussion about what had happened when we met up afterwards as we were both happy to draw a line under it and move on. I don't hold a grudge and neither does he. Our friendship was never quite the same, though, which was a pity.

The party fell apart soon after he left. I asked Mitchell what it was all about and why they got so het up. Apparently it was something carried over from the Tottenham-Wimbledon days but he was not more specific than that. It was always quite tasty stuff whenever you played Wimbledon and we had some nasty experiences as Chelsea players when we faced them, but the Spurs lads in particular had never forgiven John Fashanu or Vinnie for two specific injuries.

Gary Mabbutt was a hugely popular figure at the Lane who had battled through diabetes to play for the club and to represent his country. He had a serious clash with Fashanu in November 1993 and, although no action was taken during the match, referee Keith Hackett asked to see the club's video. Television film suggested that Fashanu's elbow struck Gary Mabbutt in the face during an aerial challenge and he was accused of a deliberate elbow. Mabbs had a fractured eye socket and cheekbone. At one stage doctors feared he might lose his eye. It was easy to see why they called John Fashanu 'Fash the Bash', as he had been accused of physical intimidation on numerous occasions. In another major encounter, in 1988, Vinnie tackled England defender Gary Stevens, who never fully recovered from the injury to his knee. That was what Wimbledon were all about in those days; intimidation was part of their armoury. It was what you came to expect from them and they rarely disappointed.

Vinnie and the rest of the Crazy Gang didn't single out Spurs players. They intimidated everyone. Still, if I had known how deep were the scars with the Spurs lads I would have kept them apart or told them not to get up to any funny business in my house. I certainly learned a lesson that day – check things out first!

CHAPTER SEVENTEEN

MANAGING WHEN THE BENEFACTOR PICKS THE TEAM

When I was told that Doncaster Rovers wanted me as player-manager, I didn't think twice; I jumped at the idea.

Really, I needed to have thought twice!

I was only thinking that this could not only be my big breakthrough into management but also extend my career yet further. Once again, I didn't do my homework, but was far too eager to take the chance. I didn't have a clue what I was letting myself into when I signed a two-year contract.

Mark Weaver, the CEO, sold the club to me, telling me of their ambitions and my role as player-manager with a view to becoming the new manager. It was too good to be true. In my mid-30s I should have been old enough to know that if it is too good to be true then, invariably, it is too good to be true.

I asked Mark to send me the contract through before I went

up to Doncaster and I should have been suspicious when he suggested that I came up for the game that very Saturday. I could complete the contract there and then and take charge of the team immediately.

Just 90 minutes before kick-off in the 1996 season I signed for Doncaster Rovers as player-manager. Mark Weaver assured me that Sammy Chung was being sacked and took me to a Portakabin that would be my office. It was at this moment that Chung was told of my appointment, just as he opened the door to what he assumed was still his workspace to find I was sitting at what up until that moment had been his desk. It was, of course, excruciatingly embarrassing for everyone in the room, but it was also shocking.

That day, to my bemusement, I was, apparently, meant to be in charge, but Mark Weaver said he thought it was the best for me to observe the team. It was true I didn't know much about them, although I had heard of Paul Birch from his days at Wolves. I went into the dressing room, where I introduced myself to the team and had a chat. Then I sat in the dugout for the game, alongside Mark Weaver, and benefactor Ken Richardson was in the stand. Having been announced to the crowd as the new player-manager, for which there was some applause, but it was obvious that no one knew what was going on. I discovered later that the supporters were suspicious of anything done by the club regime. They had already been mounting protests about the way the club was being run. The BBC was also there to document my arrival with my predecessor very much in evidence. What a farce!

There were all sorts of confrontations and confusion. It was nothing short of a total shambles with muggins caught up in the middle, not knowing what was going on, but very far from being impressed. I'd met Sammy Chung before, although I didn't know him very well and I thought – as did most observers – that this was no way to treat anyone.

I had got the impression that Weaver was running the club on a day-to-day basis, but it turned out that benefactor – Richardson was pulling the strings. This had not been mentioned when I was given the offer. In fact, I don't recall Weaver ever referring to Richardson. But by the time I had got to Doncaster and after I signed myself up I got to know an awful lot about him.

No wonder the fans were unhappy. It was said that in 1995 Richardson had hired two local crooks to burn down the main stand at Doncaster Rovers as part of a plan to force the club to move to a new stadium. One of the arsonists, an ex-SAS man, left his mobile phone at the scene. The conspiracy would eventually reach the courts and Richardson was found guilty in 1999 when he was jailed for four years.

I also discovered that Mark Weaver had run the club shop before being elevated to chief executive. He would go onto to even be some kind of caretaker manager on more than one occasion. Yet while Mark was doing all sorts of jobs, Richardson was in reality running every aspect of the club.

Under those circumstances I had a predictably stumbling start to my new role as a player-manager. There seemed to be a revolving door for coaches. Every time I looked around there was one being sacked and another appointed, including at various times Dave Cowling and Andy King, all appointed by Richardson. Kingy was a mate from Luton days and sadly passed away recently, a great boss and a good man. None was my choice and I was never consulted, but merely told about the new appointments.

It was hard to tell who was doing what. Graham Carr, the father of comedian Alan, , was also briefly appointed assistant manager. Only one thing was certain and that was that Richardson was behind everything. I was rapidly finding out that Richardson was a law unto himself and he meddled in every aspect of the club whenever he fancied and did whatever he thought was best. I cannot imagine any club anywhere in the country being run the way he controlled Doncaster Rovers.

I hadn't been at Doncaster long before he began to spend hours on the phone with me, wanting to know just about every spit and cough that had gone on during the day in training involving me and the players. He was immediately making suggestions about the team. At first it was subtle. He'd say, Wouldn't it be a good idea to pick this one or that one? But it wasn't too long before it became more than forthright and he began to sound very much like he was dictating team selection.

The phone calls got longer and longer, hours and hours, sometimes going on well into the night. He went on and on, telling me who were the best players, who I should pick, trying to convince me endlessly if I dared disagree with him, which I was doing all the time. I told him in no uncertain terms that I was picking the team and that was the end of it. It was me training the players, working with them on a daily basis and I knew which players were ready for the game on a Saturday, who was in the best shape and who would fit into the tactics for any one game. I am sure that was not what he wanted to hear and he began to look for ways of getting rid of me.

Richardson one day announced that team selection would no longer be my sole prerogative. He made a point of saying that under no circumstances was I able to select Paul Birch. Paul was the kind of bloke who would speak his mind and I guessed he must have told Richardson to F-off or something similar. Paul himself then told me that the club had decided they were no longer going to pay him. This sort of incident was common – I was working in an environment where one person would say that someone else had told them something and that somebody else would immediately contradict them. It was enough to drive anyone crazy.

Paul was desperate. 'I need the money, boss,' he said. 'I've got to be paid as I've got a mortgage.' He made it clear he would put up with not playing so long as he got paid. This was no way to run a football club. It would have been comical, if it wasn't so tragic.

Richardson threatened not to pay other players if they didn't do well. Football is often said to be a pressurised world but these were truly intolerable working conditions. We were forever calling in the Professional Footballers' Association (PFA) to mediate for the players.

I'd had enough of it all, and told Richardson what I thought of him. 'I think it's a complete disgrace. The players have negotiated contracts, they are due their money. If you want to run the team, come out and say so. Get rid of me if you want to pick the team.'

I've no doubt that this was his wish, but he knew he couldn't sack me as a player. Instead, he continued to make coaching changes and everything he did simply made matters worse and caused more problems.

I got to know quite a few people in Doncaster, many of them supporters of the club. Their feedback was interesting and provided quite an eye-opener. Much of what they were telling me tallied with my own personal experiences at the club. The locals wished me good luck and said that I would need it. By now I knew what they meant.

Eventually, Richardson put the club into administration and at last a deal could be done with the players and with me. I was able to leave the club with 12 months of my contract still to run, but I didn't want to walk away without letting the fans know why I was going and how I felt about things. I told the story to the newspapers, including how the club 'benefactor' was the one who wanted to pick the team. I am sure this was what the fans suspected in any case. The articles in the local press caused plenty of waves, which was my intention. The whole of the town was very supportive of me once I went public.

Most clubs would act defiantly to rubbish such claims of interference, but not Doncaster Rovers, not Ken Richardson. He not only picked the team for the next game but plonked himself on the bench between the substitutes and newly hired coaches. Not surprisingly, Rovers lost. They lost the next game at home to Exeter too, a result which dropped them to the foot of the table where they would remain for the next eight months, and eventually the club went down into the Conference.

I stayed in charge for just three games of the 1997 season – involving an opening-day defeat at Shrewsbury, an 8–0 League Cup pummelling from Nottingham Forest and a 5–0 home loss to Peterborough – before moving on. In total, I appeared in eighteen matches for Rovers in the old Third Division, scoring three times before I finally retired from league football. As

Doncaster's player-manager, I had fifty-two games, of which we won fourteen, drew eleven and lost twenty-seven.

In 1998, John Ryan, a Mancunian with a season ticket at Old Trafford, rescued Doncaster. I later met the new chairman and was pleased that Doncaster had ended up in good hands. He invited me to United as his guest. I also got to know Sammy Chung and realised what a nice guy he was, underlining how badly he had been treated while he was manager at Doncaster. I apologised for the way that his exit had been managed and said that if I had had a clue what was going on I wouldn't have taken the job. Sammy appreciated my honesty. He knew what I had been going through as it had been the same for him.

I still look out for Doncaster's results and wish them well. My time with them hadn't gone well for me but it had been my wish to move into management and, although it was certainly an unusual experience, at least I got an eye-opening insight into the perils of trying to run a team.

For a short period afterwards, I played for Basildon United in the Essex Senior League managed by a friend, Dave Cusack. I picked up a hamstring injury stretching to score a goal against Great Wakering Rovers in what turned out to be my last game for the club. After that my career would consist of coaching, playing and managing in various capacities for clubs such as Borehamwood, Letchworth FC, Dunstable Town and Hitchin Town.

CHAPTER EIGHTEEN

LIFE AS A LANDLORD

Among those who tried to buy Doncaster Rovers while I was there was Anton Johnson. Like Ken Richardson, he was a controversial club owner. But I got on much better with Anton who, with his partner Dave Cusack, whom I played for at Basildon, had interests in a number of businesses including several pubs. Among them was a Dunstable local called The Distillery. Anton suggested that I look at the pub with a view to running it for him.

My first impression was that it was pretty run-down but I thought it had great potential. Anton, who felt he was doing me a favour, persuaded me to take The Distillery on for three months from October 1997 to see how it went. I was to be the manager at first and, if I liked it and felt comfortable, he would make me the landlord.

During the trial period, I felt good. I learned everything from pulling pints upwards and I found I enjoyed running a pub. Anton said he would lease it from the brewery and allow me to continue being in charge. I employed Allison Duke, who had run the pub before and knew her way around. That was a huge help and we ran it effectively as joint managers, although it was now in my name.

I ran the pub for about eighteenth months and I must say I did have a great time, at least at first. I was also player-coach at Borehamwood with Bob Makim as their manager and we finished second to Kingstonian in the league. Phil Wallace was an excellent chairman and went on to do the same job at Stevenage. On the field I was still enjoying my game and having a good time. I enjoyed coaching and playing and I was happy enough even though I wasn't earning a fortune.

I got paid for three roles by the club: for the use of my name (acting as a sort of ambassador), for coaching and for playing. Each category paid £200 a week. This was a drop from Doncaster, where I had been earning £900 plus bonuses. But this was an exceptionally good non-league team and it was great to play for the love of it; I really did enjoy it.

Friday nights, though, started to become a problem. As the landlord I was up pretty late on regular Fridays, and when there were lock-ins (periods when a pub is locked so that customers can go on drinking privately after closing time) they were invariably on those nights. The next day I would have to be up for the game. Allison made sure I could have an early night if I was playing on the Saturday. She had run this pub before so it was easy for her to step back in. Bob helped by giving me plenty of flexibility and letting me know in advance if I was in the team on the Saturday, meaning I would curtail my social drinking.

It was in The Distillery that I met Kim, who was often in there with her friends. It was a very sociable pub and I really enjoyed it there. Kim had no idea I was a footballer when she met me. She went on to join the staff and years later we got together. She has gone on to become my partner and my rock and in the three months I was in prison in 2015 she visited me as often as she was allowed.

I made many new friends in the Dunstable area because of the pub. I worked hard to get custom and turn the place around. I brought in a very popular DJ, Mick Fontaine, and we ran disco nights on Friday, Saturday and Sunday. But even with a good crowd in, we had to shut at 11.30 p.m. under the old licensing laws. I came up with a right out-flanker, which we called 'pub-to-club'. People would say they were off from the pub to the local nightclub, go out of the front door and we would shut for an hour or so, perhaps even less. Everyone would then return through the back door, which was now the 'club' entrance.

The club had no till and no money was exchanged for drinks; instead, we would just write down the drinks orders. Allison was experienced behind the bar as well as being my co-licensee and she would adjust the takings in the morning. Sometimes the club would go on to four or five in the morning, but not always with me if I was playing football on Saturday with Borehamwood and made sure I went to bed early enough.

Everything was going smoothly and everyone was happy until the police came to the pub – on the day Michael Owen scored his wonder goal against Argentina in the 1998 World Cup Finals in France, two years after Glenn Hoddle left Chelsea to become England manager. The pub was rammed, people spilling out through the front and back doors, and it was hardly a surprise that this drew the attention of the police.

Officers asked me how many people we had in the pub, but it was clear we were packed to the rafters with people even filling the back garden. The atmosphere was brilliant; there was not a sign of trouble, just everyone having a great time. The police insisted we would have to get rid of some of our customers.

I said, 'Help yourself.' There was no way I was going to tell one person they had to go, while another could stay. It would have been grossly unfair and, if anything, might well have caused trouble. As it was, the atmosphere was electric with everyone singing England songs and enjoying the big game.

The police opted to leave things alone – the right move – and stayed outside, monitoring the situation. The whole place erupted when Owen scored and I could just picture similar scenes in pubs and clubs all over the country. But there were no problems even though England eventually lost on penalties in a game in which David Beckham was sent off when England really deserved to go through.

I had wanted to create a good atmosphere in my pub and at that moment I knew I had succeeded. It had become a really good football pub. Pub-to-club became legendary in Dunstable.

I had about six months to run on my contract with the brewery and was offered a twenty-five-year lease when I got a nasty shock. They demanded both a business plan and £40,000 up front. I simply didn't have the money, and had no way of coming up with anywhere near that amount. I was already running into financial trouble as it was, having got more than £5,000 behind in beer sales. The overheads were mounting. I had four or five staff to pay, partly to cover for me when I had football commitments, plus the disco, the DJ and the doorman.

As the debts mounted, the brewery began foreclosure and demanded £10,000. I just didn't have it. So they set a date by when I had to quit the pub – they were shutting me down. It was tough to take. They organised a relief to take over from me until they reallocated the lease, issued a writ for damages and that was the end for me at The Distillery.

Despite this blow, I decided that I would try to pursue the landlord career. Eventually I found another suitable pub, a place in Hatfield called The White Hart. Like The Distillery when I first took it on, The White Hart was badly run down, but it didn't take long to knock it into shape and I brought with me my staff, Allison, Karen, and Lorraine. Could I make it with this second chance? I hoped so.

It may seem strange, but I remained keen on being a landlord even after I had been injured when I tried to break up a fight in another local pub called The Bull. This was a great little place where we used to go drinking after The Distillery had closed down. It was run by Wendy Tucker. Known as 'the Duchess', she was very good to me and used to let me stay upstairs when I couldn't get back home. So when two blokes once tried to attack the manager I told them to leave it out, at which they waded in with four of their mates. Along with my friends Howard and Eric, I tried to stop the attack and got hit in the face with a glass for my troubles, leaving a big circle wound. You can still see the scar on the side of my face, close to my eye.

I met many interesting characters as a landlord and had many escapades as a result, far too many to detail in one book. One of those characters, however, set me on a path that I should never have followed. I had become friendly with one of the regulars at The Distillery, just as it was closing, and he went on to help out at The White Hart for a time. As is often the case with pub regulars, I don't think I ever knew his real name. But everyone else called him 'the Dude'.

I was still involved in non-league football when I started taking cocaine. I had never previously taken any drugs so it was, perhaps, a surprise that I fell so easily into the habit at the relatively late age of thirty-nine. But Friday nights had become a huge effort, with that routine of staying up late in The White Hart before playing in a match on the Saturday afternoon. I had noticed that other people could stay up as late as I did but never seemed to be anywhere near as tired, or to feel the effects of the late nights that certainly caught up with me.

I started to discuss the late nights with the Dude and some of his mates. I only knew the Dude as one of the punters in the pub and was horrified when he suggested that I should try cocaine. I told him in no uncertain terms that I didn't take drugs, had never taken drugs and had never contemplated taking drugs.

For me as an athlete, drugs carry connotations of cheating – even those that aren't performance-enhancing – and, although I was in the late period of my career I was still trying to keep in shape. I never cheated as a player and would never cheat. The game meant, and means, more to me than to do that.

The Dude suggested that a little sniff of cocaine would not do anyone any harm and would help me combat my fatigue during the late nights. Okay, I thought, let's give it a go. It sounded innocuous and it wasn't a drug aimed at improving my game. I took a snort and at first there was no effect. I wondered what all the fuss was about. I didn't think much of it.

I went back to try it a few times and eventually I was able to stay up a bit later without feeling any ill effects or fatigue; nor did I have the heavy hangovers I would normally get from a late-night drinking session.

That night was the beginning of a habit that would continue on and off for the next ten years. If I stayed up late drinking socially on a night out, especially before a game, I would take cocaine as well as part of the ritual. Fortunately, I have found that the urge has died down in recent years. As I no longer play and no longer have too many late nights, the need for cocaine hardly exists and I've managed to shake the habit off.

But at that time, cocaine was always readily available, although taking it was an expensive pastime – a wrap or gram could cost anything from £40 to £60 (about £65 to £95 today). I was earning a reasonable amount from the pub and from football, but I also had a lot of expenses with Michele and the kids at home. But I was still paying all my bills – just about – and losing the rest on the horses.

I wasn't really much at home in those days, or for much of my life during my time in football as the game takes you away from home so much. I was somewhat settled at Chelsea, but became less so with the moves from Southampton to Doncaster, and then the long hours as the licensee of a pub. I often had to sleep on the premises. I had been with Michele for twenty-eight years. She was the mother of my three kids, and I was determined to try to maintain a good relationship between us all. With all the money I was spending on betting and running loss-making pubs, the last thing I really needed was to be splashing out on cocaine. To make matters worse, I was still being chased for £10,000 owed to the brewery from my days running The Distillery. It was a living nightmare for me, trying to sort out financial issues that seemed never-ending. And it was becoming too much to cope with.

I hadn't been making much money from The White Hart and not long afterwards I moved out. I looked around at other potential venues, as I liked being a landlord and felt I had the ideas to crack the trade. But in 2000 the brewery had me declared bankrupt, and that meant I could no longer hold a licence, ending any hopes I had of continuing the career.

I had enjoyed my time running pubs, despite the occasional bad moments. It was great for socialising, and I met some interesting characters and made long-lasting friendships. I also looked on The Distillery, in particular, with pride. I'll always feel that I helped to make it one of the most popular pubs in the area. As for the Dude, one day he just disappeared, and I never saw him again. But then, that was probably a friendship I was better off without.

CHAPTER NINETEEN

BACK TO THE BRIDGE – MY SPIRITUAL HOME

Players these days continue well into their thirties but when I was at my peak the age of thirty was considered to be some sort of mystical number, an age at which we were just supposed to retire. But I was happy to play on, no matter how far down the football pyramid I had to go to get a game. I certainly think you need to love the game to play until the age of forty-four. It was never about how much I earned. It was a real and lasting passion for the game that drove me on.

Players sometimes quit because they wouldn't dream of dropping down one division. Not me! I dropped division after division, and I was to end up playing Sunday morning football. I didn't care about the level, I cared about playing good football and enjoying it, wherever it was, and at whatever level.

I went to Letchworth as joint manager with Johnny Alder.

I was attracted by his reputation; he had run local teams and been highly successful for some twenty-five years and he also ran a successful Sunday team, St Joseph's. I played Sunday football for them for two and a half years in the National Cup and had a wonderful time in what was a highly successful stint at that level. Decent young players included Zeema Abbey, who went on to play for Norwich, Dean Walker, Carl Spring and Jason Huntley, all making for a good standard of football.

I must say, it was sometimes complicated turning out for Letchworth on a Saturday and St Joseph's on a Sunday, but it helped that the same guy ran both teams. If he told me I'd be substitute on the Saturday for Letchworth or he was resting me then I'd be able to turn out on the Sunday.

These days, it is noticeable that players like Wayne Rooney may be advised to step back into midfield to prolong their careers, in much the same way that Ryan Giggs did at Manchester United. There have been some centre-forwards who have tried playing at centre-half and done very well, such as Gerry Armstrong and Chris Sutton. I had a go in the Letchworth reserves but while it was okay when the ball was in the air, it wasn't so easy with eager young whippersnappers running around my heels. Fortunately, at that level, most passes played forward were over the top, which I could deal with. Route one was the norm for this style of non-league football. But it was quickly apparent that it wasn't for me and I gave up playing at the back.

We won the league at Letchworth, then I moved on to Hitchin Town under Andy Melvin in the Ryman Premier League. I went on to be joint manager with Robbie O'Keefe as manager, and it was at this time in 2002 that I heard about a falling-out between Peter Osgood, one of Chelsea's greatest players ever, and Ken Bates.

Osgood, who had also played for Southampton just as I had, scored 150 goals in 289 appearances for Chelsea. He was at the club for eleven years over two spells in the 1960s and 1970s and was revered by the fans, helping Chelsea win the FA Cup in 1970 and the European Cup Winners' Cup a year later, after beating Real Madrid in the final. He had so much talent, so much going for him and he was such a wonderfully gifted individual, but he also had a tempestuous side to his character.

He had been in a PR role at thc club for nearly eight years, doing match-day hospitality for which he was paid something like £10,000 a year. Of course, old boys such as Ossie and me needed the cash, but I am sure he loved what he did at Chelsea. He even had a lounge named after him at the Bridge – but that counted for nothing when you got in an argument with the chairman. It didn't matter who you were, you were out. Four years later Ossie died, aged just fifty-nine, after a heart attack he had suffered while attending his uncle's funeral.

After Ossie had left, Stamford Bridge's Carol Fare called me about the consequent opening in the club's hospitality suites. To me, it was a dream come true, and even if it was sad to follow Ossie, it wasn't something I was going to turn down. I was already working with Chelsea TV and Big Blue Radio as the club branched out into the media. I was also doing quite a bit of punditry for Sky and the BBC. The media approached me on a regular basis to comment about Chelsea, who were always in the news for one thing or another. It didn't pay a huge amount, but combined with everything else it kept me ticking over nicely.

I did meet-and-greets on match days and sometimes took part in Q&A sessions in the lounges. I expanded the concept to invite players from opposing teams and the club encouraged me to exploit my connections within the game. If West Ham were the visitors I'd bring along Frank McAvennie; if was Liverpool, then it would be Paul Walsh; Arsenal, Kenny Sansom, and so on. I continued to run my sessions over the next twelve years, and it proved a wonderful way of extending my relationship with the club I loved so much. Even better, after I had been in the job for about a year Ossie patched up his differences with Bates and came back to Chelsea. He and I worked in hospitality together and became good friends. It was a pleasure working alongside him. He was a good man, as well as a wonderful player.

CHAPTER TWENTY

SNIFFER DOGS AND CHANNEL 5

It is early May 2014, 8.30 a.m. I'm in bed, lying next to my partner Kim. We are in her house in Dunstable.

Kim thinks she hears a knock on the door... and then there is a bang.

She gets out of bed, there is another bang and I throw the covers back, about to leap into action, but before we know it the room fills with twenty coppers and five sniffer dogs. Outside is a Channel 5 film crew. What on Earth are they doing there?

The police said they were acting on a tip-off from a member of the public. I could only think it was someone with an axe to grind, but I was baffled as to who it could be or why they would want to make such a call. The search of Kim's house turned up a solitary wrap of cocaine. Even the police said that it was of low value, and we admitted it belonged to Kim.

Nevertheless, they cuffed me and said they were arresting me on suspicion of supplying drugs. I told them they were making a mistake.

I was just as shocked to find tripod-mounted TV cameras outside our home. It was clearly a set-up. It was bad enough that all these coppers and sniffer dogs had come crashing in, without TV cameras following their every move. One of the TV crew asked me if I minded being filmed and interviewed. I told them to get lost. *Did I mind being filmed*? Of course I bloody minded!

I was taken to a cell, and from 11.00 a.m. to 7.00 p.m. I lay there looking at the ceiling. During all that time Kim was trying to tell the police that the wrap of coke belonged to her, but nobody listened. In vain she repeated that it was for her personal use and I was not dealing, that there was nothing more to it.

Inevitably, it was in all the papers the next day and the damage was done, even though all charges against me were eventually dropped in September. Kim received a fine for possession and a warning. But the mud stuck, and the immediate repercussions were dreadful. It dawned on me that my life was beginning to unravel and that I would lose my position at Chelsea, who couldn't be seen to be employing someone facing drug-dealing charges. But there was worse to come.

CHAPTER TWENTY-ONE

ROCK BOTTOM

That same May, Kim and I were heading back late one evening after I had been working in London. It was just a week after the police raid. We had been the subject of extensive media coverage ever since, which wasn't surprising since Channel 5 had turned up with the police it was clear the media had been well-informed. The allegation that I was dealing drugs was a load of crap, but the media fell upon it portraying it in a way that was hugely damaging. And if anyone missed it in the papers it was all over the Internet. It was hugely embarrassing for both of us to be on the receiving end of this treatment.

Chelsea stopped using me on the club's TV channel, which was bound to happen even though the charges against me were later dropped. This was so unfair and also, I thought, completely out of proportion. But that evening Kim and I just wanted to unwind, away from all the nonsense. We should have bought a few cans and gone home. Instead we thought we would park up at home and take a taxi to The Nag's Head in Dunstable, the only pub in the area open after 11 p.m.

Big mistake.

Our intention was to stay for a couple of pints, no more. We needed a bit of cheering up and we knew the place well; we always ran into friends there. Having ordered our drinks we began to unwind and to forget our cares. I went to the toilet at the same time as two other blokes, one of whom looked to be pissed. They were at one end of the urinals and I was at the other.

One said to me, 'How you doing?'

When I looked up, the man said, 'Are you the drug dealer?' I ignored him but he persisted, 'Well, are you? Have you got any?'

'Listen, mate, leave it out,' I said. My tone meant business. 'Do yourself a favour and do one.' We went back into the bar where he joined a number of his friends in another corner, ordering lots of drinks. I didn't know any of the faces.

Some time elapsed, maybe as long as a couple of hours. While we were elsewhere, the pissed bloke – I later learned he was a builder – reappeared and sat in Kim's place, her bag still at the bar, where we had been sitting. I asked him to move somewhere else, politely, but got no response. He sat there, holding his pint glass in his hand and I worried about what he might do with it if things got ugly. I still had the scar on my face from being glassed about ten years earlier and I was very worried about something similar happening. I repeated my request.

'Fuck off, fatso,' he snapped.

I finally lost it. A combination of the fear of being glassed and having to endure his foul-mouthed taunts set me off. I whacked him in the face. He swayed a bit and I hit him a few more times. I kicked the glass out of his hand, in case he tried to use it on me. He went down on the floor and stayed down.

Kim picked up her bag, I spoke with the bloke behind the bar and told him I was going, and he said, 'No problem.'

We went twenty yards down the road and turned into a narrow, dark tunnel. Kim said, 'Look out, they're coming, they're behind you.' Two blokes, one with a glass in his hand, ran towards me. I whacked one and kicked the other. One of the attackers was the man I'd hit in the pub. Clearly he wasn't too badly hurt to come after me – I found out afterwards he had a cut lip and some loose teeth. The pub's doorman ran over to us and another couple of lads ran out to help. Eventually Kim and I got home, but that was not to be the end of it.

The police later took the CCTV footage from the pub and took matters on from there. I was playing in a Chelsea legends match at Orient when they arrived the first time, but I was able to finish the game as they didn't know where I was. I was eventually arrested, held in a cell for an afternoon and charged with assault causing actual bodily harm. The police also went to my parents' house. My dad was furious with me, as you would imagine, and he was right to be.

In June 2015 I was found guilty of actual bodily harm and I had to accept it. I had hit the man, and I hurt him. But the judge ruled that the jury was not to take into account the events that occurred outside the pub, all of which had been captured on film. That upset me, as that evidence was proof that those guys were out to get me. But I do now understand that this was beside the point. I am ready to make sure that this never happens again, rather than dwelling on the past and fretting about whether what happened to me was fair or not.

Loads of people were prepared to go to court to speak in my defence or testify to my good character.. The PFA wrote a supportive letter, as did Chelsea, but these didn't influence the outcome. The judge made it clear that she felt I should have walked away from the incident, irrespective of the provocation. She had a point, but having been glassed at The Bull I was terrified at the prospect of it happening again. I felt I had acted in self-defence.

I was ordered to return to court to hear my sentence, and the judge told me to prepare myself for a custodial term when I did so. I thought that I had at least a 50-50 chance of staying out of jail. The probation officer to whom I had been assigned had recommended community service and a suspended sentence, and I reasoned that as it was my first offence I might be okay. But it turned out I was deluding myself. I was handed a nine-month prison sentence.

CHAPTER TWENTY-TWO

LIFE ON D-WING AND E-WING

Quite simply, prison was the loneliest place I have ever been.

Being sent down happened so quickly, so that it was all a bit of a blur. When the judge read out my sentence I couldn't hear her properly so I asked the officer by my side what she had said. The answer was, 'You've got nine months. Come this way.' That was it.

My son, Joe, passed on my bag, and that was it. Kim had already left the court. She couldn't bear to hear the sentence so I didn't get to see her. My barrister, Mark Wyeth, said he was sorry and that he had done his best, but I had been punished in a fair manner and I knew the consequences. Of course, it is a bit galling when you hear of so many other worse crimes attracting far shorter or more lenient sentences, but that's the way it is.

I was put in a prison van and told we were going to Bedford, but the worst part of the journey was the sweat box I had to squeeze into, for these vans contain a number of small compartments for prisoners in transit. My shoulders and knees touched the sides and I found it extremely oppressive, made worse by the heat. I started to have a panic attack and they told me the air-conditioning would be coming on. I felt like I was in a coffin. But we travelled for a full forty-five minutes before the air-con kicked in, by which time I was in a state. I realised that I was claustrophobic. A dish of water was passed under the door and I gulped it down. As a means of transporting prisoners it was horrendous, and in my opinion it should be changed, for it is inhumane.

I spent the first night in a cell on my own after being kitted out with prison clothes. The inmates working on reception when I arrived gave me some chocolate bars and I was given the opportunity to make a two-minute phone call. I let my dad know where I was and told him that I was okay, even though I was far from being so.

I was in a remand rather than an open prison, and it was not a soft touch. In my playing days, we all used to joke about a 'welcome to hell' when a team went off to play in a hostile environment. That was nothing. This was the real hell.

I didn't know what lay ahead for me. It was a weekend and it wasn't long before one of the warders came into my cell and told me to pack up all my things – what few there were –and sent me off to D-Wing.

I was shown to a cell, where I was greeted by a large, muscular bloke, and the first thing he said was that he didn't want me in there with him. Trust me, he didn't look like someone you'd pick an argument with. He said he was awaiting sentencing and he didn't fancy sharing his cell with anyone. I stood by the door, holding all my stuff, completely taken aback by what was going on. I said to the officer that it was fine by me if I went elsewhere, but she replied that the cell's occupant would be on a report if he refused. She had a private word with him and I was in.

He was sitting on the bottom bunk, so it was pretty obvious I was on the top. I didn't think there was much of a choice. Considering his irritable mood, it wouldn't have been wise to request that he moved bunk. So that's where I went, top bunk. And straight to sleep.

We did eventually get talking, as there wasn't much else to do, since we were locked up for much of the day. He told me his name was Cyrus and that he was in for armed robbery. And that was about as much as I got out of him.

I found out a little more about Cyrus from others. I was a bit shocked to hear that he targeted post offices, and I didn't ask for details. Best not to, I thought, however curious I might have been. I did discover, though, that his mate Tony, who presumably did the armed robberies with him, was on the same wing. He was actually quite a good bloke and I ended up playing backgammon with him.

It wasn't long before the loneliness kicked in. It was an awful feeling, and it started to take its toll. It didn't help that Cyrus loved the TV programmes that I hated. He would sit there watching, to me, crap such as *Storage Hunters* and *Jeremy Kyle*. Until then I had never heard of *Storage Hunters*, and quite frankly never want to hear of it again. Both shows drove me to distraction, but it didn't seem sensible to argue with Cyrus, although by now we were getting on okay.

I was assigned a personal officer named Miss Gill. She told me what to expect during my time in prison, and was very helpful in the first weeks, especially as the terrible feelings of loneliness started to affect me badly. She said that if I took on some work I would be paid, and added that she would keep me informed if anything came up. I told her that I was prepared to do anything to alleviate the boredom and ended up taking a cleaning job. Any time spent out of the cell and away from Cyrus and his TV shows was a godsend. On the Tuesday, four days in, I had a visit from my son Joe, for which I was extremely grateful as he brought me news of what was happening on the outside. He was great, and it was really good to see him. He told me that Kim, Mum and Dad were okay, and that my outstanding bills had been paid.

The highlight of my prison day was the half-hour when all the inmates were allowed to get some fresh air in the exercise yard. Despite its name, there was no greater exercise on show than strolling around in circles, but the chance to be out in the open air was heaven for me, and I loved that period, no matter how short. It allowed me to get some sunshine on my face and it felt so good, a small taste of freedom. The period always seemed even shorter than thirty minutes, and it would be called off if it was raining. At least it was the summer, so it didn't rain too often. I also loved watching all sport on TV, when I could prise Cyrus away from his reality-TV shows, that is.

I applied for a tag, which would get me out of the prison early, although it entailed home detention with a curfew. But that was a small price to pay for getting out of there even a day or two early. To qualify, I had to have served ten weeks of my sentence, with good behaviour.

Cyrus was sentenced and there was an item on the TV news about the armed robberies he and Tony had committed. Cyrus got thirteen years and Tony fourteen. There wasn't an awful lot to say to Cyrus, apart from to sympathise about the length of time he would be inside. Here I was, thinking that nine months was a long time.

One of the wardens, Mr Afeez, enrolled me into a football quiz in which the prison officers took part, but I must confess that I didn't do too well at guessing the results of games. But I loved daily visits to the gym. I lost a considerable amount of weight and got my fitness up to the point I where I was running for fifty minutes on the treadmill and could even manage 400 press-ups. There were a couple of officers in that gym, Dean and Paul, who were outstanding. I didn't get special privileges but they treated me very fairly. Every bit of kindness helped.

I was disappointed when my first application for a tagged early release was turned down, but I was told that it very rarely, if ever, happened at the first attempt. I immediately applied again.

An old friend, Clive Brown, was on E-Wing, and he suggested that I should try to join him. There were bigger gyms and more lads into fitness over there. Also, by now I had had five different cell 'mates', and the latest one had started to smoke in the cell, after having promised not to. I successfully applied for E-Wing, where I met two great lads in Scott and Ruly, alongside Clive, Edgar, John and others. I continued with my cleaning job, and also began to serve food each day. I went to the gym every evening, and as a result was spending less of the day locked up in a cell.

At night I played cards with cellmates Scott and Ruly.

Sometimes we played pool, too, although not in the cell, of course. I had never won at pool before but in prison my game was improving. Scott and Ruly wrote me a kind letter when I got out, saying that when I left the cell it was never quite the same. I'd like to thank both of them for helping me get through it all, and I wish them all the best.

A few of the lads liked their football and we would pass the time by guessing the winners in the Premier League. I would regularly come up with seven out of ten. The one that let me down was Chelsea. I kept on picking them to win, and they kept on losing.

Until I got to prison I had never heard of the drug 'spice' (also known as 'fake weed'), but quite a few inmates were taking it. I was never offered it and wouldn't have taken it if I had been, although I saw wardens raid cells with sniffer dogs. There was also a suicide during my sentence. Someone hanged himself in his cell, went into a coma and could not be revived. I never knew the guy. Why would he have done it? Well, let me tell you, when you're inside you can understand why. You appreciate the depths of depression that take hold. It's easy to slip into feelings of being unwanted and unloved, coupled with loneliness. I know, I felt it for myself. It was undeniably a shock to my system to feel such emotions.

Strangely, my lifelong gambling addiction and its consequences actually helped me, in a perverse sort of way. I'd taken so many knocks and had learned to fight back. You needed a similarly thick skin in prison, needed to be able to cling to some sort of belief. I knew that I never wanted to return to prison. I clung to that belief and it kept me going. Kim had visited on the Thursday, two days after Joe, and Mum and Dad came soon after. I spoke to Kim on the phone every day, and my sister Jane, also a rock in my life, visited as well.

At length I applied to become an enhanced prisoner, and was put through for a job in the library. That proved very helpful in my final six weeks, as there were also two lovely librarians, Sally and Monica, there. I had also been allotted a much better cell, although I still suffered from the claustrophobia and panic attacks that I had first suffered during the sweat-box ride from the court.

I would look out of my cell window, gasping for air, wanting to get some space, pushing myself as far out as the bars would allow, having opened the window the fraction that was possible. It was both terrifying and uncomfortable, and left me feeling overwhelmingly anxious.

I might have hoped that while I was inside at least the rest of the world would leave me in peace. Not a bit of it, for I received a threatening letter from the legal-aid system claiming that I owed more than £5,000 in legal fees and that the bailiffs had been called.

I was appointed a duty solicitor who applied for legal aid on my behalf, but it was declined because I had been receiving fees from Chelsea until I went to prison. I had £1,000 a month from the club and a pension of just £5,000 a year. My total income was £300 a week and once I'd paid my bills there was nothing left. Yet here was a debt-collection firm hounding me – even while I was in jail. It made me even more anxious. They threatened to turn up at my home and take away whatever they could find. But I didn't own my own home, I lived in Kim's house, and I was worried that they would try to take things from her. I felt my life was caught in a downward spiral, and depression kicked in. My solicitor, James, told me not to worry and said that he would write back contesting the claim, although the debt agency continued to send me letters.

As part of my bankruptcy I had a trustee looking after my financial affairs, and he proved to be very good. He prepared a summary of my income (not very much, and virtually zero after Chelsea stopped paying me when I was jailed) and expenditure ahead of my discharge as a bankrupt in January 2016.

I did sometimes receive letters that cheered me up however. David Pleat said that he remembered me as a kid wanting to be a footballer when I grew up, and his words were immensely comforting to me. And he wasn't the only one who wrote. Visits from my loved ones also became more important. Kim came as often as she could, as did my boy, Joe and my parents, and my sister Jane. I realised how important my daughters Kelly and Gemma are to me, irrespective of everything else. I had plenty to reflect on. Mostly on how I had ended up in prison, the injustice (I believed) of the court case, the gambling that had left me penniless and how these problems reflected on my family and friendships. My family had stuck by me with fierce loyalty, but I had lost so many good friends – not because they hadn't stood by me, but because I had asked too much of them, put them under far too much pressure to help me, leant on them and in doing so, asked them for one favour too many.

Gambling, though, was the root of all the evils. It had left me penniless, it had made me desperate, it had led me into dangerous situations, and it had driven me to make so many wrong decisions. Gambling led to me breaking the law and – however much I felt I had been hard done by – much of the self-reflecting I did in prison made me realise that I had driven myself into this position.

One example of my law-breaking was drink-driving. I am totally against it. And yet I have done it on occasions when, because of my gambling, I found myself without any money, having had a drink late at night and being unable to pay for overnight parking or a taxi home. How stupid could I be? But that's how low I went. Thinking about it in prison, I realised that, now, I would rather go without a night out than contemplate getting behind the wheel of a car.

My second application for tagged release was finally successful. Kim was paramount in making sure it went through, having done all the checks on the paperwork. It was a condition that I had to stay at my parents' house for three weeks, and to be indoors at set times when I would be checked. I was so grateful for my parents allowing me to stay. It wasn't great, given all the restrictions, but it was a damn sight better than remaining in prison.

I had been in prison for three months and three weeks when a warden told me it was time to pack my bags. It didn't take long and I couldn't wait to get out and see Kim. Joe was to pick me up in his car.

As I was walking out of those doors I made the decision that I would never be returning. The experience of being in prison had dramatically changed my outlook on life, making me realise that I need to walk away from potential trouble, however much someone may try to get a rise out of me. That said, I still think that I shouldn't have to endure being provoked, in a bar or anywhere else, while going about my own business. If people have nothing nice to say to someone, they shouldn't say anything at all, however well-known the other person. No one deserves to be treated that way, whoever he or she may be.

Leaving prison was an amazing feeling, like scoring in an FA Cup Final (not that I did), or netting a winning goal to receive a medal, or seeing one of my babies born. It was all the most wonderful things in my life rolled into one.

The first thing we did was order the one thing in prison that I had dreamed about most of all – curry. Followed by the kind of chocolate pudding I used to love at school. Then I went home to my parents to sample some of the other normal things in life – fresh air, walking around the local fields, the sheer joy of freedom and the sensation of being able to shut the door behind me without it being locked. I also had to have a tag attached to my ankle. But that was a small price to pay.

CHAPTER TWENTY-THREE

REBUILDING MY LIFE

Alvin Martin had been in the World Cup squad of 1986, and now he was speaking in front of two hundred corporate guests at a lunch in the City. He was taking the piss out of me, and also in the audience were some former players I'd known: Ray Wilkins, Frank Stapleton, Graham Roberts, Ossie Ardiles, Mickey Hazard and Rob Lee, as well as cricket legend Mark Ramprakash.

I loved it. It was the football banter I'd missed. This was my first public appearance since being released from prison five weeks earlier, in the autumn of 2015. It was my first opportunity to meet up with some of the lads again and it felt good. Even the jokes at my expense put the smile back on my face. It made me feel a whole lot better about myself.

I had Steve Surridge from Eclipse Sports Promotions to thank for inviting me, and for organising my attendance at a couple more dinners. He has been fantastic since I came out of prison, as he had been while I was inside. One of the nicest men I've ever met, he's been a friend for a long time.

West Ham player Mark Ward was also at that City event. It was good to talk to him, as he too had been to prison (for possession of cocaine with intent to supply), albeit for a much longer time. I was encouraged to see how he was rebuilding his life. He wrote a book to help him draw a line under what had happened to him. Perry Groves was there, as well, another who had visited me in prison. On my release, he helped as much as he could in trying to get me some work with personal appearances, and had also become a very good friend.

There was the temptation to overindulge at that lunch with the wine flowing freely, but I resisted it. I have made a conscious effort to turn over a new leaf and to make something of my life again. I was never a heavy drinker, but I wanted to be sure I didn't start now. I want to do the right thing, and to maintain the right attitude. I want to do what is right by my family and friends. I want to be sure I don't let down those who have recently helped me so much, people like Gary O'Reilly, who had helped me when I was down and out, before I went to prison, by getting me work as a labourer. It's at times like those that you learn who your real friends are – when you are so far down that you have nowhere left to go. It's not always about how much money someone can give you or lend you. Sometimes good advice and being pointed in the right direction are just as important, and valuable.

Almost the first thing I did when I came out of prison was to make arrangements to see Bruce Buck, the Chelsea chairman. I will always naturally gravitate toward Stamford

Bridge, I have always considered myself connected to the club and its supporters. I loved my job in the hospitality lounges, on Chelsea TV and as a pundit, and nothing would have given me greater pleasure than regaining the position I lost, unsurprisingly, when I went to prison.

Kim accompanied me to a lunch meeting that also included Bobby Barnes from the Professional Footballers' Association, who has been extremely supportive all along. Bruce was encouraging and made the point that I would need to be seen as a Chelsea legend once more before anything else could be considered. I understood exactly what he meant, and it made me all the more determined to become that person again. I came out of the lunch with fresh hope.

I am sure I helped to give Chelsea fans some wonderful memories, but they are nothing compared to what Roman Abramovich's investment, and consequent success, have given them now. I think of the incredible No. 9s since my day – Drogba, Hasselbaink and Costa; traditional No. 9s. I would love to be part of the Chelsea set-up again, if it's possible.

It's often said that you don't really appreciate what you have until it has gone. I had been grateful for the work I had been doing with Chelsea, but perhaps I should have been even more appreciative. I understood their perspective on my position now, following my release from jail, and were I to be given a second chance back at the Bridge I would be sure not to let them down.

When I next saw Bruce Buck it was on the very sad occasion of the funeral of Bobby Campbell. I had heard of his illness after I got out of prison and had called him on his mobile. His wife, Sue, answered. She told me that Bobby's eyes lit up when he learned it was me, and it made me feel good to know that. He still had his wonderful sense of humour. Sue said he asked, 'Why didn't you call for the last four months?'

Despite the reason for our gathering, it was great to see so many from Chelsea at the church. The football 'family' is often talked about, but rarely has any real meaning. At Chelsea I think it is different, and I could feel it at Bobby's funeral. There were managers and prominent Chelsea supporters. I spotted one of the lads I knew from the club's tour office, as well as Elvis and Ledgie, tour guides at Chelsea I had worked with. Bobby Barnes came from the PFA, and players included Graeme Le Saux, Ken Monkou, Jason Cundy, Damian Matthew, Gareth Hall, David Lee, Graham Stuart, Frank Lampard with his fiancée Christine Bleakley, Frank Lampard senior, Harry Redknapp and David Pleat, among many others. David shook my hand and said, 'Get yourself sorted and you'll be okay.'

He was not alone in showing a willingness to help me at my lowest ebb and I want to use this opportunity to thank all of those who have done so. Old friends from school and later have stood by me, including Les, Mick, Denis and Eddie, all four of whom visited me in prison. I hope to repay them by staying strong and continuing to make something of my life.

Troy Deeney got his second chance with Watford. He deserved it; he had served his time, and his life needs to go on. Each case must be judged on its merits. I've heard that said many times, and for some it happens, for others it might not. I've read of Troy saying just that, and I agree with him, because if nothing else I believe that I have come out of prison a better person for the experience.

EPILOGUE
BY HARRY HARRIS

Second chances. How many can one human being expect to be given? One, two or three second chances? It cannot be endless.

Kerry Dixon has had plenty of second chances, but his nine lives have run out and now it's his last chance.

Having written more than seventy football books in a career spanning over forty years, I can truly say this is the most amazing story of its kind that you are ever likely to read. That said, however, it is time for Kerry Dixon to move on, to rebuild his life, and in this he will need some friends and allies to help to put him back on his feet. He knows there are no more chances.

Paul Merson felt as though writing his book with me was part of his therapy and, listening to some of his experiences, I reflected that it must have been awful to have been him during his darkest days. Yet some of the incidents in his life were too brutally honest to include in his book, as they would have deeply hurt loved ones. But if you rolled all the books about those who have hit rock bottom into a single volume, that would be the life of Kerry Dixon.

There have been a number of players who have gone to prison and returned rehabilitated. Watford captain and Premier League goal-scorer Troy Deeney is the latest. He is frank about the person he once was, and relieved, as well as grateful, that he was given the chance to become who he is now – a husband to his long-time partner, a father to two children, a feared finisher who scored sixty-five league goals in the previous three seasons, helping Watford as the captain and driving force of the newly promoted side. Having been jailed for ten months for affray, he was released early because he had demonstrated his remorse in court and in prison, and because it had been his first offence. Kerry Dixon was also jailed for his first offence. Like him, Deeney emerged from prison a changed man. He played for Watford ten days after his release with an ankle tag, which he had to wear during games. It had to be wrapped in padding and approved by the referee before every match.

Quite a few players preceded Kerry Dixon to prison. Arsenal and England captain Tony Adams served fifty-seven days in 1990 for drink-driving. He successfully returned to the game and later founded the Sporting Chance charity, which helps sportsmen with drink, drug or gambling addictions. Former England, Arsenal and Crystal Palace striker Ian Wright, now a TV pundit, owned two cars but did not to pay insurance or road tax on either. He was sentenced to fourteen days in prison. One of the greatest players of all time, George

Best, was an alcoholic. In 1984 he was convicted of drink-driving, assaulting a police officer and failing to answer bail, and was jailed. Sadly, alcoholism eventually caught up with him, leading to his death in 2005 at the age of fifty-nine. Joey Barton was twice convicted on charges relating to violence. Liverpool legend Jan Molby missed three months of the 1988–9 season when imprisoned for drink-driving. When he got out of jail he was straight back into the first team, and the following season helped Liverpool win their eighteenth League title. The Welsh footballer Mickey Thomas was at Wrexham in 1993 when arrested and convicted of counterfeiting and money laundering. Duncan Ferguson led Everton to their 1995 FA Cup victory over Manchester United, but off the field faced four charges of assault, three of which resulted in fines. West Brom striker Lee Hughes was behind the wheel when he crashed his Mercedes in 2004, killing a passenger in the car he hit. He was convicted of causing death by dangerous driving and leaving the scene of an accident, and was sentenced to six years in prison and banned from driving for ten years. Mark Ward was arrested and charged with possessing a class-A drug with intent to supply. He was jailed for eight years.

It seems to me that Kerry Dixon deserves a second chance as much as any of those names. He has unburdened himself by telling his story, having suffered in silence because not even half the truth has emerged in the media. He has spent a great deal of time going through the detail of his life, with often painful honesty. Footballers' obsessions and addictions are easy to comprehend, and they are far more widespread than the fans might appreciate.

Kerry has had a tough nine months since being released from prison. He needs to prove himself all over again, to become what he should be – a knowledgeable and respected pundit on the game, and one day soon, I hope, back at Chelsea. I am confident that he can make it. I believe that readers of his story will be, too.